PROTECTING EURASIA'S DISPOSSESSED

A Practical Guide for NGOs Working on Issues of
Forced Migration in the Former Soviet Union

The Forced Migration Projects of the Open Society Institute were established to monitor circumstances in different regions of the world in order to provide the international community with early warning of forced movements of people, and to identify the social, economic, and political conditions which cause such dislocations. The Projects encourage early and effective humanitarian responses to migration emergencies; advocate the humane treatment of those unable to return; urge permanent solutions for those displaced; and promote measures that avert individuals' need to flee. The Projects gather information concerning displacements and the circumstances that motivate them, concentrating primarily in 1996 on the 15 countries of the former Soviet Union, the former Yugoslavia, Haiti, and Cuba.

The Open Society Institute is a private operating foundation that was established in 1993 to promote the development of open societies around the world. Toward this goal, OSI engages in a number of regional and country-specific projects relating to education, media, legal reform, health care, and human rights. In addition, OSI undertakes projects aimed at encouraging debate and disseminating information on a range of issues which are insufficiently explored in the public realm.

Forced Migration Projects Staff:

Arthur C. Helton, Director
Laurence Berg, Information Coordinator
Françoise Girard, Associate Director
Elisabeth Socolow, Assistant Director (Prague)
Susan Poncher Willis, Executive Assistant

PROTECTING EURASIA'S DISPOSSESSED

A Practical Guide for NGOs Working on Issues of
Forced Migration in the Former Soviet Union

Open Society Institute
Forced Migration Projects
888 Seventh Avenue
New York, NY 10106 USA

ISBN 0-9641568-2-2 Paperback

Published by
The Open Society Institute
888 Seventh Avenue
New York, NY 10106

Produced by Michael Vachon
Designed by Kimberly Iowaka Barber
Text set in Adobe Garamond by David Cote
Cover photo: © James Hill, refugees from Georgia

TABLE OF CONTENTS

PREFACE

This report is designed to encourage non-governmental organizations (NGOs) to work on migration-related issues in the former Soviet Union (fSU). The intended audience includes policy
makers and NGOs, primarily those headquartered outside of the
region, which are considering the establishment or expansion of
activities in the region. The specific objective of the NGO work in
question concerns population displacements.

The occasion for the issuance of this report is an unusual
international conference process, the Regional Conference to
Address the Problems of Refugees, Displaced Persons, Other
Forms of Involuntary Displacement and Returnees in the
Countries of the Commonwealth of Independent States (CIS) and
Relevant Neighboring States, which is to take place in Geneva in
May 1996. A unique Programme of Action being drafted for
issuance at the conference, as well as the conference process itself,
will undoubtedly encourage NGO work in the region. This report
is offered as a long-term resource for organizations considering an
initiation or expansion of activities in the region.

Since 1991, more than 5 million people have been uprooted
by the conflicts and changes occasioned by the dissolution of the
Soviet Union. Hundreds of thousands reside in crude, temporary
shelters waiting out the wars in the Tajikistan, the Caucasus, and
southern Russia. Roughly 25 million ethnic Russians are living
with uncertain futures in republics outside the Russian
Federation, anxious about the possibility that, one day, they will

suddenly feel pressed to emigrate.

With over 130 ethnic groups in the fSU and nationalism, secessionist movements, and discriminatory measures in evidence, the potential for further dislocation in the region is enormous. Official systems responsible for meeting the needs of those forced to flee are embryonic and easily overwhelmed. Resources in the independent sector are diffused and non-governmental organizations are still in formation. In the meantime, suffering and loss of life result. Strengthening of the role of NGOs in the former Soviet Union is an important objective, not only because of these organizations' contributions to resolving migration and refugee problems, but also because a thriving independent sector inherently strengthens the growth of civil society and helps prevent the causes of forced migration.

The upcoming regional conference on migration-related issues in the countries of the CIS could put regional issues, including strengthening the capacity of NGOs, on the agenda of the international community and assist policy makers and donors in their efforts to address new responsibilities. A comprehensive, regional approach would include preventive and post-emergency strategies to address the evolution of humanitarian action from relief to rehabilitation as well as the promotion of respect for fundamental human rights. To encourage maximum participation by the independent sector, the Forced Migration Projects initiated an informal conference preparation process, encompassing local and international NGOs, independent experts and policy makers. Meetings to assess the situation of NGOs and exchange information were conducted in Almaty, Kiev, Moscow, New York, Novosibirsk, Tallinn, Tbilisi and Washington, D.C. This report is one product of this process.

During the past few years, experts in the field have watched the rise of a broad array of local and national groups, associations, and foundations dedicated to issues as varied as physical disabilities, revival of national literature and heritage, women's rights and gender issues, and the resettlement of people uprooted by ethnic conflict and economic turmoil.

The proliferation of groups working in so many endeavors is an encouraging step in the gradual evolution of an open society. While the focus of this report is predominantly forced migration and refugees, it strives to set these issues in the context of the burgeoning NGO field.

The break-up of a unitary state in the twilight of the twentieth century poses a host of unprecedented challenges to the successors, including the reformulation of legal and institutional frameworks, including a new regime of international treaties. This, compounded by the sheer complexity of the Soviet Union's past of forced deportations and labor migrations, requires a reconceptualization of traditional criteria.

For example, this report deals not only with issues pertaining to classic refugees, as defined under the terms of the international refugee treaties, the 1951 Convention and 1967 Protocol relating to the Status of Refugees, but also with the more voluminous population of internally displaced persons (IDPs) and "returning Russian-speakers"—some of whom no longer feel welcome—who were born in or settled in non-Russian republics.

Similarly, the emergence of a whole new sector of "non-profit" groups—voluntary organizations created and operated outside state control—is something without precedent in Soviet history. Not surprisingly, in the midst of a chaotically privatizing economy, the traditional definitions of "public charity" and "non-profit" are often difficult to identify in practice. For purposes of this report, the Forced Migration Projects have therefore followed the lead of NGO workers in the region in adopting a slightly more ambiguous definition of "NGO."

Micro-enterprises are a good case in point. A group of IDPs or returning refugees who need to rebuild their homes, for example, might form a micro-enterprise "NGO" to repair local buildings that they found destroyed by war. The micro-enterprise, however, could be profit-making. Or an international relief organization might help a local NGO refurbish a defunct factory in order to produce the blankets needed by tens of thousands of IDPs. That project might be profit-making, but it would serve the IDPs at a fraction of the cost of buying the blankets elsewhere and shipping them to the affected population.

Of necessity, this report touches upon a varied set of factors relevant to population displacements. This ranges from conventional emergency assistance, protection, local integration and repatriation, to include development-oriented measures needed to stabilize a region and prevent forced migration. The report also takes into account the work of human rights monitors, legal services and legislative policy advocacy, as well as preventive measures such as citizen-initiated conflict prevention and reconciliation. The fundamental organizing principle, however, is the coerced movements of people.

This report is one of a series of special reports. It is based on a mission of inquiry conducted in March 1996 by Kathleen Hunt, a writer and consultant, under the auspices of the Forced Migration Projects of the Open Society Institute. Ms. Hunt, a former Moscow correspondent for National Public Radio, is a visiting scholar at the Harriman Institute of Columbia University, and is finishing a book on the post-Soviet transition. She is the principal author of this report. Assistance in research and the preparation of report appendices was provided by Debra S. Cooper, a lawyer, Elisabeth Socolow and Françoise Girard of the Forced Migration Projects, and Eliana Jacobs and Christian A. Nielsen, graduate school students and interns with the Projects.

Ms. Hunt spent the period from 2-16 March 1996, conducting research in Moscow and the southern republic of Ingushetia, home to thousands of Chechens and Ingush displaced by conflict. More than 36 lengthy interviews were conducted with international and local NGO officials, as well as international relief and monitoring groups. Prior to the field research, Ms. Hunt interviewed 25 individuals involved with humanitarian work in the fSU. To maintain confidentiality, interviews and queries were conducted with the understanding that observations would not be attributed to the individual speaking, but to a general category such as an "NGO official," or "an expert with several years of experience working in the former Soviet Union."

The lists of NGOs in Appendices I and II were selected from thousands of entries in a number of lists and databases. However, they cannot hope to reflect an authoritative compilation covering the vast ground in this changing and expanding field. They do, however, reflect a concerted effort to survey the local groups known in the former Soviet Union, as well as those based in the West, involved with migration-related issues. Queries were dispatched to a wide array of organizations and individuals on three continents, including the European Community in Brussels and Moscow, and the bilateral aid headquarters of the leading Western donor countries. Many furnished us with information on their work with local NGOs, and that information has been incorporated as appropriate.

The bibliography, legal analysis, and list of laws in Appendices III, IV, and V are designed to provide basic references for those planning to establish or expand activities in the region.

The research for this report was conducted independently of the Open Society Institute or other entities or foundations supported by George Soros. Certain OSI offices have been listed in the appendices, however, when other NGO sources identified their programs as relevant to this report. The Forced Migration Projects apologize to any organization whose work with refugees, migration or related issues escaped our notice. At the same time, the Forced Migration Projects have not knowingly listed any organization which has abused the status of "NGO" for purposes of conducting activities unrelated to human rights, migration, refugee assistance, NGO development or advocacy. Inclusion in the lists, nevertheless, does not imply an endorsement in any respect by the Forced Migration Projects.

The Forced Migration Projects wish to acknowledge specifically the generous cooperation of the Armenian Assembly of America, Center for Civil Society International, Eurasia Foundation, InterAction, Save the Children Federation, Swedish SIDA, United Nations Development Program, USAID, World Bank, and World Learning in furnishing the lists of grantees and partners throughout the newly independent states.

Despite the abundance of NGOs registered across the Eurasian continent, one field which is conspicuously under-served is the very topic that concerns this book: forced migration, including refugees. It was therefore gratifying in the course of the research conducted for this report to receive encouragement and support from numerous individuals who welcomed the prospect of the addition of this report to the literature of the field.

The Forced Migration Projects sincerely thank the many people in the field—local citizens and expatriates—who untiringly answered queries and offered their insights and experience. Their generous assistance is a testimony to the dedication and energy that will foster the development of open societies.

Arthur C. Helton
Director, Forced Migration Projects
May 1996

12

CHAPTER ONE

THE RISE OF NGOS

The Goals of Local NGO Development

The Forced Migration Projects believe that NGOs can play a more active role in the development and observance of humanitarian law in the countries of the fSU—addressing issues of citizenship, refugees and migration. The reasons are many. Local NGOs, even in their formative stages, are in a unique position to perform very useful functions in both the short and long term.

For the immediate future, as international resources dwindle, small-scale local NGOs can be highly efficient at providing some services that the economically strapped states cannot—or simply do not—provide.

In the matter of forced migration and refugees, these services must address the pressing needs of hundreds of thousands who have already fled their homes during the last nine years and furnish creative support to help those who want to stay where they are. Examples of such local NGO initiatives are the "self-help" migrant enterprises which have appeared among the returning Russians and citizen-based conflict prevention programs that have emerged in ethnically tense regions.

Local NGOs also have a potential role to play in providing independent information and encouraging critical thinking among the general population, whose main access to information is often state-run television. Again, in matters of refugees and forced migration, lively NGO publications and creative media programs could raise awareness of the laws that exist in their country as well as the rights of citizens and others. Through the media and the burgeoning electronic mail networks, NGOs could aim to dispel dangerous rumors and propaganda which can spiral with frightening speed into conflicts and dislocation.

In addition to becoming new sources of information, local NGOs in fields encompassing human rights and forced migration should strive to participate in policy making and planning, areas that were previously the exclusive domain of the government. In those republics where large numbers of the population are contemplating emigration, local NGOs can work with the authorities to forge programs aimed at inducing people to remain. In regions where immigrants have already arrived, local NGOs can often be more effective than the state in easing resettlement and adaptation to new surroundings.

In the long term, a maturing NGO sector can urge the government to be more accountable to its people, and eventually strengthen the rule of law and civil society. Only through such a process, which likely will be lengthy, will concepts such as human rights, freedom of expression, and tolerance of diversity come to be put into practice. Putting them into practice will, in turn, mark an important step in the prevention of forced migration.

With relation to foreign donors, independent local groups are often excellent guides to many close-up issues pertaining to migrants and refugees, and can be of great assistance to outsiders whose exposure to the former Soviet republics has been limited until only recently. Their insight into the local social, economic, and political reality can help identify and address the preconditions to conflict or environmental disaster, which can lead to population displacements.

Antecedents to the NGO Sector

As former Soviet citizens will repeat like a mantra: the Soviet state ran everything, including the social safety net. But to newcomers that fact can be hard to visualize. This is particularly so for veterans of international aid programs accustomed to working in settings where some form of community-based voluntarism functions—be it in constructive counterpoint with a democratic state or in open opposition to a repressive regime. The significance of this "missing sector" cannot be overstated. Nor can the legacy of the centralized Soviet state, party, and security apparatus be discounted, with its baffling maze of overlapping, competing, and contradictory jurisdictions at the federal, regional, and local levels, throughout the former USSR.

Period One: Forced Volunteerism

Until the end of the 1970s, community participation for Soviet citizens was obligatory. Everyone "volunteered" to clean up their neighborhood on Saturdays in the state-organized *Subbotnik* rituals; everyone "voted" in general elections; and everyone joined the Young Pioneers in grammar school and graduated to the Communist Youth League in secondary school. Dependence on the Communist party and Soviet government was simply inescapable, and some now say they performed these required functions with only half-hearted enthusiasm and cynical distrust of the state.

Those who were sincere about their participation—and there were many indeed—were still taking part in a structure that was organized from the top down. Loyalty to state and party certainly inspired many of them, but it is a mistake to think of this impulse as stemming from the same roots as the Western notions of citizens' rights and duties. These concepts of citizenships took shape in societies which were defining themselves in part by their independence from the state apparatus. In the USSR, by contrast, the development of individual initiative was not a goal of state and party-sponsored organizations.

Nevertheless, there were, albeit under some "all-Soviet" umbrella, shades of local initiative in the form of local stamp collectors' clubs, pet enthusiasts, and even groups who slipped away to the forest during summer weekends to hold folk-music fests. But a more consequential development for the future NGO sector proved to be the early association for environmental conservation, founded in 1960 by university graduate students concerned about protecting Eurasia's abundant natural resources. Known as the *Druzhina* movement, these conservationists planted the seeds of the future environmental movement which flourished in the late 1980s as nuclear and chemical disasters struck cities, remote villages, and towns.

Period Two: Glasnost Spawns the Neformaly

The mid-1980s heralded another phase of the Soviet regime, which began with the social and political "openness" inaugurated by Mikhail Gorbachev and continued until the decisive year of 1991. Members of local NGOs recall the close of that decade as a time when the state began to feel its weakness and permitted small community groups, albeit with suspicion, to supplement diminishing social and health services. A flurry of groups appeared, called at the time *neformaly*, ranging from political discussion clubs and environmental activists to associations of Afghan war veterans.

Many of the groups were extremely informal, as the title suggests, operating out of the members' small apartments, and adamantly striving to be independent of the state. In contrast, others were not so independent and had considerable budgets and spacious offices allotted by officialdom. In time, these came to be dubbed "GONGOs": government-organized non-governmental organizations.

GONGOs came into existence in a variety of ways. Some were formed by the state in an attempt to co-opt the more independent-minded elements in society. Others were formed as parallels to the more independent groups, to compete with them for invitations to international conferences in the relevant field.

Still other GONGOs evolved from the myriad extra-curricular organizations sponsored by the state and party, such as the *Komsomol*, which recognized and seized the emerging opportunities for contact with foreign delegations and potential for funding and travel. Their staffs were often quite polished, highly competent in Western languages (atypical for the average Soviet citizen), and had impressive ties to people in the powerful state and local ministries. Consequently, they were often the Soviet citizens most accessible to visitors to the USSR during the days of *glasnost.*

Period Three: Entering the Post-Soviet Age

Toward the end of 1991, with the approaching demise of the Soviet Union, NGOs took off in a sprint, especially anticipating the massive Western aid promised to ease the transition to a market economy. As local NGO officials describe it, the early 1990s ushered in a more cooperative relationship with the state, which was weaker than ever, acknowledging the need for charities to help fill big gaps in services. During the chaotic period from mid-1991 through the first year of President Boris Yeltsin's rule, the state even provided office space in public buildings to selected NGOs.

Some of the local non-governmental groups which sprang up like crocuses during 1992-93 gradually came to approach the Western notion of voluntary organizations, and a few began working with members of the Russian parliament to draft new legislation on the status of charities and non-profit organizations.

Strangers Meet

During this period, Western donors seeking to work with the new NGO sector discovered sharp cultural and legal distinctions between the Western voluntary sector and the muddle of post-Soviet organizations. Against the backdrop of the "new Russia," where nearly every prominent political figure was regularly cited in the local press as profiting from state-owned real estate and foreign joint-ventures, no one had ever set standards for drawing a clear line between public and private, commercial and charitable interests. (Some difficulties which arose from this disjuncture in perception are discussed in Chapter Two.)

Since 1992, the loosening of state control over matters of public life has reduced some of the prevalence of the "GONGO" phenomenon (at least in Russia), but as a former human rights monitor recently remarked on returning to Moscow, a new phenomenon is the "Potemkin NGO," i.e. those which are merely facades. A Potemkin NGO's staff may also appear extremely professional, proficient in several foreign languages, and impressively connected to key officials in the administration.

Without exception, the warning from dozens of experts in the field is: Know with whom you are dealing! It is worth taking the time to establish this clearly, even if it takes months to meet with the local group being considered, and to consult with experienced local and international people.

One should not presume, however, that every group with a polished staff is a Potemkin NGO. The majority of the more active local NGOs are true NGOs in spirit, even if many lack the administrative and fundraising characteristics common in the West. But a hybrid sort of NGO has evolved as well, generally regarded as a medium-term phenomenon, which combines small-scale entrepreneurship with more traditional non-profit service activities. If once subsidized by the Soviet state, or able to support their community activities on the state salaries they collected, many local NGOs now find themselves adrift and feel compelled to introduce a profit-making element to raise money for their programs.

To complicate matters, perhaps in reaction to a past of totalitarian control, many ordinary people tend to apply the label "nongovernmental" to any activity that is not organized by the state, including local small enterprises. In Tajikistan, a foreign aid official described some groups as being "more like small business clubs, trying to clean up the shambles of the war and get some sectors of the economy running—not 'do gooders' or humanitarians *per se*." The result is that, for the time being, local and international NGO officials seem to have settled for the fuzzy line between pure voluntarism and entrepreneurism. But again, they are quick to warn prospective donors to get to know their potential partners carefully.

The Future

The preceding has been a brief summary of the telescoped evolution of NGOs in a society that had no real precedents for public charity and voluntarism. As described in Chapter Three, this process is rolling like a tremor across the continent, with the bulge still mainly located around Moscow, and barely a ripple felt in the farther reaches of Russia or the former republics. There is great turnover every few years and, in the Darwinian competition for dwindling foreign funds, some organizations will thrive, others will merge with like-minded groups, and others will fold.

It is crucial to bear in mind that in a population of nearly 300 million, the notion of voluntary participation is still a foreign idea. Those who expect a huge surge of participation in grassroots organizations will be disappointed. But the activity has been impressive, nonetheless, and some building blocks to more diverse and open societies are in place.

CHAPTER TWO

THE LESSONS LEARNED: 1990-PRESENT

"You talk about freedoms that took centuries to debate in the West, through logical steps, but this country never went through that progression. You talk about implementing a 'sack of democracy,' but of course you can't implement it. In our training programs at Charities Aid Foundation, we divide democracy into 1500 components such as being a responsible human being, coming to work on time, answering and returning phone calls, saying 'thank you,' holding the door, and having respect for others' rights. We teach democratic habits. In fact we teach components of democratic habits, and that way, avoid playing to nationalist sentiments."

— *Russian NGO Official, Moscow, March 1996*

In the Beginning

To land at any airport in Moscow during the transition from Soviet to post-Soviet rule was to plough through a crush of voyagers, traders and confused men in uniform. Travelers seemed to sail through customs carrying crates and baggage containing months of food commodities, major appliances, and all manner of office equipment. Met by friends outside, they were whisked to a place in the city—a private apartment or a modest office recently allocated by the government for a pittance to certain non-profit groups—and set out to work by the seat of their pants.

Some new foreign NGOs found apartments, usually through local friends and budding counterparts. They offered to clean it up for the landlord, tested the phone, plugged in the fax and laptop, and set to work. Often they did not wait to hang a shingle, and began the tortured months of paperwork required to register with one of the plethora of federal and city organs. Local friends—or partners in their field of activity—often brought in bright young people as staff candidates, and for the next year they worked devilish hours, foraged for food, and griped about the winter mud and spring slush.

"The Period of 'Anything Goes' is Over"

Gradually, the authorities got around to clamping down on customs and income taxes, and cries of protest rose from both the business and non-profit communities. But the authorities stood their ground, and as a Western grants manager firmly stated this winter, the period of "anything goes" is over. "Anyone operating on that basis is making a very, very big mistake and doing a huge disservice to the whole effort of non-governmental development. After all, the object of NGO work is to strengthen open societies."

Of course, he continued, adherence to tax and customs law has a painful effect. As a donor, it raises your operating costs; as a recipient it cuts into your operating budget. But given the emergence of a healthy skepticism in the former Soviet Union about the value of work being done by Western foundations, there is all the more need to be more concrete about what one wants to achieve there.

There was a time, probably most vivid in the late 1980s, when the people of the Soviet Union threw open their doors to the long-forbidden foreigners then walking their streets, and the farther one ventured from Moscow, the longer this period of welcome lasted. But signs of the ambivalence and inner turmoil gnawing away at daily life were detectable as early as the end of 1991. Even the emergency humanitarian aid shipments to help the dazed republics through their first winter of independence met a mixed response: gratitude from the poorest, and humiliation and resentment from the patriots.

Likewise, the multi-million dollar aid programs and accompanying arrival of Western program officers in 1992 and 1993 raised the hackles of those in the former Soviet republics who had been demanding all along that money be sent but Western staff be left back at home. That gulf has become even more pronounced—in salaries, in living conditions—and continues to provoke criticism from both local and Western quarters. It is a gulf continues to feed the frequently muttered cynicism expressed in the conviction that "the foreigners come here only to make money, even though they say they're here to help."

According to aid officials still working in Russia, much has changed and the grace period when Russians sought Western leadership is over, although perhaps in the provinces people may still be open to guidance. There is a much more sophisticated attitude among Russian non-governmental organizations, as well as within the Russian government, toward Western philanthropy. In theory, this should make it much easier to work. But it also makes it all the more important now that the Western organizations operating in Russia and elsewhere in the fSU be completely transparent and compliant with the law. This is the view shared by responsible NGO people, both international and national: "Register. Pay your taxes. Do things above board."

Facing the Bureaucracy

All NGOs are required to register and pay their taxes. But these, and scores of other bureaucratic rituals vary from place-to-place and from time-to-time, often without warning. Permits and stamps that took days to obtain to satisfy one set of rules may inexplicably fail to pass muster in another jurisdiction. This is especially true in the case of forced migrants and displaced persons, for whom several bodies of evolving law exist—international, national and local—but whose daily fate can be decided by yet another local edict or decree pertaining only to a particular place.

The puzzle of permits and paperwork becomes more complicated for NGOs working in conflict zones. One of the searing lessons has come out of the most dramatic humanitarian crisis still unfolding in Russia's war with Chechnya—the imposition of arbitrary documentation requirements from the ministries of interior and defense. Without warning, NGOs have been blocked at checkpoints for lack of a permit or special stamp, which they are told they can obtain only by going back to the regional authority or all the way to Moscow. During periods of Russian offensives, as recently as March 1996, foreign NGOs—even the International Committee of the Red Cross (ICRC)—were blocked from bringing assistance to Chechen civilians under Russian bombardment, in apparent violation of the principles of humanitarian law as well as the formal agreement between ICRC and the host government, which establishes ICRC's right to carry out its mandate.

Public Perceptions and the Collision of Cultures

Given the unfamiliarity with traditions of charity and voluntarism, it is taking time for the former republics—leadership and citizenry alike—to learn the history and norms of the international humanitarian community (for example, the integrity and neutrality symbolized by the red cross). Local people can still be confused about all the groups that drive the white four-wheel-drive cars with symbols and names written on their doors and carry radios for their own security.

The absence of traditional charity and volunteer work in Soviet society has left its impact deep and wide. All NGOs working in the fSU, particularly outside the major cities, report widespread ignorance and skepticism of the voluntary sector. The following experience of one program, which set up an NGO center in a conservative region of the fSU rarely visited by internationals, capsulized the complexity of local attitudes toward NGO work.

The program emphasized training of nascent civic organizations in management, computer use, and policy advocacy, and soon after it was set up the center published a newsletter. The staff found a lot of interest among the local participants, especially on how to understand and defend their rights.

But in the community at large, the response had a dark side, reflecting one of the more alarming developments since the glow of *glasnost* dimmed: local suspicion of humanitarian organizations. According to the frustrated program director, "Local people don't understand what we are. We're not business. We're not government. We say we're here to 'help the people.' They say, 'Yeah, sure! Be honest, why are you *really* doing this?' They have no concept of this kind of work, no tradition. They think we're spies."

Suspicion, springing from ignorance, often spawns another perception that undermines the goals and spirit of voluntary efforts: foreign organizations have "deep pockets." This poses difficulty in ferreting out NGOs with sincere purposes from other "NGOs" seeking personal and business gains through affiliations. The phenomenon is understandable in view of the economic and social conditions constantly shifting like sands under foot. But it does not make it any more pleasant for the NGO when the "deep pocket" assumption lurks beneath the surface or attracts people who would join up with an NGO only for self-interest.

Adding to this the lingering GONGO-legacy from the Soviet era, one NGO official emphasized that "the situation is so complex. You have a lot of governments and industries setting up NGOs because they understand that this is the way to get money." But pointing to a positive development, she added that it is possible to find a good ex-government person who runs a real NGO. Still, the process is stressful. "I worry about it all the time. You always face the risk that someone has ulterior motives."

Destructive motives of self-interest can flourish in a setting such as the fSU, where the tradition and standards of non-profit work and monitoring are unknown. One donor working for years with local NGOs in Russia points out that if one is doing small business development training, proximity to commerce is so great that the possibility of conflict-of-interest is greater. But if one is working only in an area such as human rights, on the other hand, the possibility of corruption is less obvious.

Nevertheless, the risk of conflict-of-interest is solidly built into social habits as well as into Russia's 1995 legislation on non-profit associations, which allows NGOs to make profits as long as they are ploughed back into their organizational activities. There is no guarantee that this clause will be abused, but it is worth being especially vigilant.

Coping With the Paradoxes

Legion are the tales, petty and grand, of conflict-of-interest and nepotism and, more often than not, the most disconcerting feature of these tales is the local counterpart's failure to recognize the conflict-of-interest in what has been done.

A concise illustration of this is the case of a Western NGO official who came to Moscow for a couple of weeks to finalize plans for retaining a local representative in the fSU. His trip, in the dead of winter, was typically packed with meetings from dawn till midnight, dashing around to offices for registration paperwork and talking continuously with the fellow who was his likely candidate for the position.

Throughout his stay, he stressed the rules of transparency, legality, and the importance of finding ancillary staff, such as a deputy and book-keeper, who would do everything above board. Together they continued the paperwork and the search for a part-time bookkeeper. Finally his departure date arrived and he met once more with his new counterpart to tie up loose ends. What about the book-keeper? he asked. "I have a perfect solution to this problem," the Russian fellow answered, sending a shiver of relief through the exhausted foreigner. Who? "My wife!"

Such scenes are bound to unfold across the region, and donor organizations say they must strive to make the process of the work as fair and transparent as possible. NGOs who conduct grant competitions have had the most success when they have traveled far and wide, first to inform local communities of the program and seek out appropriate local NGOs for the competition. Then they take time to explain the application process extensively, and work with the applicants while they are drafting project proposals.

And still, as one director of an NGO support center far from Moscow explained, it was necessary to tell the staff, when they were conducting a grant competition, that they could not give applications to some organizations and deny them to competing ones; they could not hand out information about grantees to rival applicants; and they could not allow competitors to photocopy applications already submitted and then underbid them. It takes time to learn on both sides, she said.

Another piece in the counter-intuitive puzzle is the missing word for "accountability" in the Russian language. The closest term is *otvetstvennost*, which simply means "responsibility," and lacks the stronger connotations of accountability.

Fortunately, with the degree of decentralization that has taken place in politics, more local governments are increasingly accountable to the local population. Local NGO representatives say that there is a bit more understanding of the relationship between elected officials and locals. Occasional training seminars now teach local citizens how to track down the voting records of their representatives in the Russian Duma, and how to make the politicians more "accountable" to them.

Money: You Can't Live Without It, But You Can't Live With It

One of the most challenging lessons learned by donors and others working for several years in the fSU is the vexing ambivalence toward money. For local NGOs faced with daunting needs in every aspect of life, saving kopeks to buy a pad of paper, a quick infusion of money in the right place would seem obvious. But it is not always positive. This is a realm in which the counter-intuitive seems to thrive. Given the official prejudice against money preached by the Soviet regime, many people have such impassioned and contradictory views about money that they might even be prompted to say that money is evil. There are several features in local NGOs (some self-defeating) that help explain this.

Sanctity of Volunteering

So many of the earlier NGOs were truly founded by volunteers with shared interests (in human rights, for example) and many heated discussions have taken place as their economic hardships worsened over whether or not to accept payment for their labor from a donor. One side of the debate argued—and still argues to some extent—that money tarnishes the spirit of a volunteer organization by paying salaries to the workers. Volunteers are a sacred category and cannot become "workers."

With time, some of the NGOs best known for this philosophy have grudgingly yielded to their donors' urging to create a more professional organization, which requires a paid director and staff. But the debate is likely to be heard for some time to come.

Delicate Balance Within Loose Organizations

Many new NGOs started out as informal gatherings of friends or acquaintances drawn together by a very personal cause. Often, for philosophical reasons, or in reaction against the dictatorial manner of Soviet institutions, they have resisted forming a hierarchical structure and make their decisions through lengthy discussion—or not at all. With few funds, they have little need for accounting and budgeting. Little strategic planning is ever done.

This balance can be irreparably shaken if one of the informal leaders receives an award for the work of the group or if the group suddenly receives a sizeable grant. One long-time NGO worker noted that "even $7,000 can create a huge uproar in a smaller-sized city." A windfall of cash not only raises the question of who will control it, but can also upset the equilibrium of an organization. Without a formal structure, decision-making procedure, or even a bank account, this can create bitter wrangling among the members, which can threaten the future of the organization.

The Cultural Bias Against Perceived "Begging"

One early NGO worker with a great fondness for the Russians with whom she has worked closely for several years summarizes the essential contradictions about money she has observed, contradictions which seem to make grant applications and proposals particularly hard to prepare. First of all, it is a great paradox, she explains, because the Soviet people were very dependent on the state and lived off money that was not their own. They all received subsidies and they indeed became very demanding.

But at the same time the whole idea of asking for money from a private foundation is very uncomfortable. It is culturally complicated to ask for money, not only because it is coming from a foreign source; it is also complicated if they are seeking support from private contributors in their own constituency.

Worse still, it is hard to ask for money on the basis of deserving it. She has often found that when her Russian colleagues were writing a grant proposal, it was particularly difficult for them to analyze and demonstrate why they were the ones who could do the project, based on the record of their former work. They felt they would seem to be bragging that they had done well.

Furthermore, she found it was an "entirely foreign concept" to ask for money and get it, with the condition of having to account for program expenditures.

Distrust and Envy

This is the harsher side of social life but one that may gnaw away at a non-governmental organization's operations. Open, direct competition is a healthy feature of a burgeoning field seeking funds from the same diminishing sources. But a number of people speak of the challenge of dealing with the less healthy rivalry and slander which takes place on a personal level. Also, some non-governmental organizations' operations workers in the field have found local staff unwilling to consider raising funds among the wealthy new businessmen because of their resentment toward wealth in general.

"That's Not What I Meant"

Some observations appear so commonplace as to be banal, but they are included here because the people who formed NGOs back in the days of the Soviet Union have harped on them again and again. One common pitfall nearly everyone notes is the mistaken assumption that a meeting or conversation is understood correctly by all sides. This is particularly common when meeting with the more educated and motivated people in the field, where it is easy to take for granted that one's own knowledge of organization-building is shared by the quite professional counterpart from a local NGO. The familiar phrases can lead to the perception of a smooth communication on both sides. But this can be an illusion, only to be dashed when the two sides realize that they both interpreted meanings that were not the meanings intended.

One NGO veteran likened the experience to imagining little "thought bubbles" over everyone's head, and trying to "read" what is really being said. The speedy rectification of any misunderstanding is strongly urged, but this can be harder than it appears. According to some who were interviewed for this report, the Soviet legacy of domineering power-relations still prevails in many settings, and foreigners may be loath to confront people with whom they are working. Such hesitation could permit a misconception to snowball.

Before Beginning a Partnership: Know Who You Are [1]

NGO experts working for several years in the fSU have found that there is nothing worse than representing their organization at a meeting to set up a group project and being unable to provide concrete answers to their partners' questions. Too often people listen to what the partner organization says it needs, and rush to convince their headquarters that they should take certain action before analyzing the potential consequences of such a choice. The organization may limit their options, and the result can be a serious loss of faith when they have to break the news to their Russian counterparts.

In addition, it is quite common for initial meetings to stir such mutual enthusiasm that the two sides lose sight of what their respective organizations can actually do. Confusion often arises, and this can hamper judgment concerning the type of organization they need to work with.

Before embarking on a partnership, veteran NGO professionals suggest taking a step back and critically analyzing several aspects of your own organization, basing it on sound management and common sense. Again, some of these observations may seem self-evident, but they derive from several years of experience in Moscow working with Western and local organizations. In fact, the following steps could equally be taken by the numerous local NGOs that are now developed enough to analyze their own structure, work, and objectives.

The first task is to draft a list of your organization's mission and goals, and then a detailed list of what it actually does as an organization and the methods it uses to do it. Once that list is drawn, it is important to add to it the activities that the organization does not do (for example, register refugees and IDPs; distribute food relief; build shelters; provide legal counseling and advocacy). This is almost as critical as the list of what your organization actually does, because it might help screen the field of appropriate partners and thus avoid serious misunderstandings.

The second issue to tackle is the manner in which your organization makes decisions. Again, draft a description of how your group is run—whether by hierarchy, consensus, or a blend of both—according to the kind of decision needed. This lays out clearly to a partner the structure of command within which you are working.

A third issue pertains to the size of your organization, as most prospective partners may have no image of size without some yardstick against which to measure it. This description should include the number of staff, the number of people served by it, and whether or not that community is static or changing in size. On the scale of NGOs throughout the United States, Europe, or the fSU, it is useful to identify where the organization falls, in terms of size, budget, and geographical area covered.

Finally, apply an acid test that can be very revealing to an NGO serious about its future development: ask if a million dollars were suddenly given to the organization to correct something in its structure or administration, what would that be? Follow that with a second question: if the organization suddenly received several million dollars for any program (either new or existing) what would that program be? Answering such hypothetical questions can help identify the immediate strengths, weaknesses, and capacities to change within an organization.

Rethinking the Aid Model

Start Small

After several years and millions of dollars of aid disbursed for developing NGOs, independent trade unions, and other sectors of a nascent "civil society," many of the people who have worked on those projects are re-considering their approach. As very few major outlays have been made in fields related to refugee and migration problems, their views reflect their experience with projects encouraging citizen participation, openness, and diversity in society.

When asked for advice for newcomers, many say, "Start small. If you are planning to form a partnership with a local group, you need to form it before the money is brought out. Build up the office gradually."

Take the negative example of an information center for NGOs that was in its planning stages. Seminars were held for NGOs to discuss the role of the information center, and soon there were debates over who would control the funds. Almost without exception, NGO professionals in Russia insist that the most successful partnerships are based on a common goal. One must discern to what extent a group is sincere, and has some history of dedication to an issue. This is especially difficult because so many groups have not been working in an organized way for any amount of time.

There are areas, such as northern and southern Siberia, that are virtually cut off from outside information and outside experience, where people are living in desperate, oppressive conditions. Yet the few Western NGO workers in such regions have found that people usually have a good idea of what they need and want to do; but they must spend time with them, to see to what extent they have the capacity to do what they want to do. To provide training before a person shows any kind of dedication is a waste, they say. And "the pressure to spend a huge amount of money on such training efforts is a recipe for disaster."

Pioneers in the NGO field agree that it is ill-advised for any donor, without extensive exposure to the region, to venture out to the provinces in search of local NGOs with which to work. As a consequence, a number of local NGOs in major centers such as Moscow and St. Petersburg have enjoyed a "halo effect," having successfully managed their initial grants and become a magnet for new donors in search of reliable partners.

Seek New Talent or Enhance Established NGOs?

The dense concentration of NGOs in Moscow—to the relative neglect of the provinces and former republics—is a matter of concern to the international donor community. Many of the civic initiatives of the last three years have been designed to render the funding process as accessible as possible and to engage the participation of local people so that new talent will surface.

But reality poses a dilemma to donors with increasingly scarce resources to allocate. Is it best to reach out in a wide sweep of regions, to find and assist new and potential NGOs? Or is it more effective, over the long term, to fortify existing "core groups" which are already the best experts in many ways, and later to support them in branching out to train and develop new NGOs?

One problem with the latter approach is that the existing "core groups" are so stretched with their own substantive work that they cannot spare the time to expand their own group in order to free themselves for training out in the field. In the field of human rights monitoring there are a number of excellent experts whose knowledge would be a boon to emerging groups in various regions, both in Russia and the other republics. But these experts are already working more than full-time simply documenting the human rights abuses in the prisons, conflict zones, and even cities such as Moscow, to train "cadres" in their own locales, much less beyond.

A Moscow-based legal clinic for forced migrants is a case in point. Every week a handful of lawyers offers free counsel to refugees and IDPs. But if they go out and conduct seminars in the regions, there will be no one to staff the center.

Most donors and international NGOs have dealt with this dilemma up to now by working on parallel tracks: fostering existing groups through seminars and material support, and exploring the regions through travel and publications. One group that has been successful in developing a grassroots environmental network, built itself up around a central core, and channeled information through regional umbrella groups. Now, the group has developed

Training: How the Trainees See It

"When Russian organizations invite foreign trainers, they often find that Americans, especially, do not know the real situation here. There are two main things a foreign trainer should know before holding seminars in Russia.

First, our social security system is very different. We have been in a country where charity was done by the state. It is still much the same outside Moscow. Foreign trainers need to know more about the relationship between the state and individual when they talk about fundraising. They never think to discuss the role of the state. Instead they talk about how to raise money from business.

Second, foreign trainers need to listen more to the people they are training, and accept what they say. It's usually a one-way communication from the side of the trainer. If they asked more questions about the reality for NGOs here, they would find out very interesting things. Often the people being trained know a lot and have such a different perspective, but they have no skills in evaluation.

Foreign trainers should try to have more respect for their audience, because these NGO people are really doing something every day, and want concrete information, not theory. They want to pull back the black curtain from the process of grant-making. They don't understand how decisions for awards are actually made and as a result, they begin to suspect that these foundations have some kind of secret purposes." [2]

—*Russian NGO trainer, Moscow, March 1996*

into a center for information and coordination.

Particularly during the past three years, training seminars have proliferated in Russia and some of the neighboring republics—covering every subject up the ladder of organizational operation from office etiquette and equipment use to grants compliance and legislative lobbying for the more advanced NGOs. On the whole, the exposure to new skills and ideas about management, program planning and fundraising is seen as very positive. But the seemingly endless cavalcade of foreign consultants conducting seminars prompted one Russian NGO director to comment that they are "saturated with training."

Year-by-year, as Russian NGOs have developed, several have established their own training programs, which are often more in touch with what people call "local nuances."

Critique of Funding System

One NGO official echoed a critique commonly heard in non-governmental circles, of the USAID practice of funding programs through independent contracting agencies which may or may not have any experience in the field. The official said that "the whole deal now is you're evaluated on the management of the grant. Twenty-five to thirty-percent of it goes to the contracting firm. USAID forces them to count the beans. You miss a bean, you're burnt." He went on to say what many others say—that there was no commitment back at "pass-through" headquarters to what is supposed to happen in the field.

The type of group this official is criticizing is distinct from the stable of Western-based organizations which have spent decades in the field doing humanitarian work. In cases where the headquarters are the direct funders and have substantive expertise with field programs, the overseas staff and their local partners do not engender these complaints.

But in this case, the official complained that the contractor had no commitment to the project's partners or to Russia. The program was micro-managed by U.S. Department of State, USAID in Washington, USAID in Moscow, and then by the contractor back in the United States. To top it all off, the official said that the goal of the project was rewritten several months into the program.

A number of observers share the belief that the brief duration of Western aid projects in the former Soviet republics (2-3 years) forces the distribution of more funds than the local setting can often absorb. Particularly in regions farther from Moscow (or other cities with highly developed NGOs), donors must have realistic expectations. The local groups are often just getting started. It often takes six months to get set up, followed by another six months focusing on training. Then the donor starts to award grants to local organizations, and has to wrap it up with final evaluations and documentation. Many shared the view that it is hard to accomplish much within the bounds of a 24-month program.

The Reality for Local NGOs

It is not difficult to understand the frustration voiced by both the internationals and local NGO personnel interviewed for this report, as regards the volume of funding and the low absorption levels of the local NGO sector. A survey done by the Charities Aid Foundation, a local NGO support center and clearinghouse, found that as many as 80 percent of the NGOs in three provincial regions had no office, and many of those that did have office space in other regions, received it from local officials. The majority had no computer, photocopy machine or electronic mail.[3]

Many local NGOs also have no bank account that can handle foreign currency from an international donor, and still others have no bank account at all. Money transferred from abroad to Russian accounts of local charitable organizations is subject to stiff taxation, so some groups have tried working through a mediator. But that can be dangerous too, as it can be difficult to know the mediator. So many local NGOs simply live with their limitations, and receive in-kind donations in the form of equipment and supplies.

The sweeping economic and social pressures during these years of transition have had a direct impact on potential—and established—NGOs. People cannot find affordable office space, and some are even being forced out of space that the state had donated in the flush of communism's collapse, as rents have doubled and tripled. People cannot afford office materials, or the phone bills which have gone sky-high. Tax laws can siphon off as much as 40 percent of their organization's income for payroll tax. People cannot afford to volunteer when they are already working two or three jobs.

In the provinces the lack of housing, office space, telephone communications, and general infrastructure are all the more extreme. Donors eager to reach out to the less-served areas might carefully consider the example, in the box below, of a Western

---

Nightmare on Komsomol Street

The situation was vastly more difficult than the field officer had expected, even with his background, which had often required him to work with very basic accommodations. After weeks of difficulty finding housing in the town where he had intended to live, he looked for a house in the nearby village. But there were no phone lines.

The place he finally rented costs more than $1500 a month, for what he describes as the "crummiest house he has ever lived in, in any country." After a break-in and robbery, it now has bars on the windows, steel doors upstairs and downstairs, and a big gate with locks. He says he lives in a jail. The surroundings are muddy lots and garbage heaps.

His program managers back in the US expected him to be up and running within six weeks, he says. In the end it took six months to find an office and get it renovated, furnished, equipped, funded and staffed and ready to do the projects. He stressed that one cannot take for granted anything: the housing, electricity, water, telephone communications, or the cooperation of the government.

The former Soviet Union is the toughest place he has ever been, he says. "I was told many things. But if I had a correct picture of the reality here I would not have come."

— *Interview with Western NGO official, Moscow, March 1996*

---

organization which sent an expatriate with considerable background outside of Russia, to set up an office. It was exceptionally rough going, and the NGO official warns others to accept that it can take half a year to get a foreigner settled and an office created.

How To Succeed Without Losing Your Mind . . . or Shirt

No one working in the ex-USSR would dare to think that a plan for success could be implemented. But in numerous interviews conducted with veterans of NGO work in Russia and elsewhere, one NGO was cited as an example of a fine grassroots effort, carefully conceived and executed. It is the American-based environmental clearinghouse known as ISAR (formerly Institute for Soviet-American Relations), which began its work in Russia in 1990, in close collaboration with the local Socio-Ecological Union (SEU). Working out of a modest apartment in central Moscow, ISAR's Russian director cites several features of their work that have enhanced their broad-based, grassroots development.

Narrow the Focus
Faced with a sprawling geographical area, it is essential to narrow the focus of the organization's work. A corollary to this counsel was mentioned by other NGO professionals, who encouraged new NGOs to choose either a subject area or one or two republics on which to concentrate.

Small Start and Keep in Touch
Since 1993, ISAR has developed a successful small grants program, through which they work with the applicants before the proposals are submitted for board review. Board members are all local experts selected for their knowledge of the subject matter and also for their experience as environmental activists. Despite the ris-

ing cost of living in the fSU, they find that very small grants can go a long way. The sums range from $500-1500 for start-up, to as much as $10,000 for efforts involving two or more groups.

When the grants are awarded, the grantee signs a contract which is written according to very specific criteria. After a grant is completed, ISAR stays in contact with the grantees. Over the course of time, they have learned a great deal about which groups are best to deal with, and built a broad base.

Since opening its environmental clearinghouse in Moscow in 1991, ISAR has provided the support to set up more than 50 resource centers which furnish desperately needed technical information to local groups and allow ISAR to follow their progress. With a strong commitment to the relatively efficient and inexpensive medium of electronic mail, they have gradually provided the grants to hook up 175 groups or sites with computers and modems.

With all this, after a stretch of more than five years of helping to build one of the former Soviet Union's most extensive grassroots networks, one of the leaders admits that there are still local groups and undiscovered talent out there that they do not know about.

In addition to the steady, small-scale measures practiced by a group like ISAR, various NGO officials mentioned other factors that play a vital role in determining success or failure.

The Power of Personality

Time and again, veterans of the NGO sector in the fSU admit that the success of a given NGO—local or international—is often due to the sheer personal power of the people involved, often the leaders themselves. A fine example of this is the experience of a woman in an industrial town south of Moscow who had adopted a number of orphans, and approached the boss of the largest local factory in town for funding assistance. She got as far as a meeting with him, but failed to convince him. At the end of the meeting, it was the close of the day, so she casually asked him for a lift home. As they pulled up to her house, she invited him in for a few minutes, "just to meet the children." Once she got him inside, he was hooked on the kids, and ended up financing her project.

Such anecdotes are common in many non-governmental activities, as well as in the collapsing public school system. Energetic principals tend to scrape up funds to run decent schools. In all these cases, the project is even more likely to succeed if the issue is personally close to the people involved.

Strong personalities, of course, lend themselves to interpersonal squabbles, and several NGO officials observed that it is useful to bring in an outsider to help resolve some contentions. They have found that having a neutral person involved can lift the power struggle or personality conflict out of its immediate context and help to resolve it. In recent years, several Russian NGOs have developed training seminars in conflict resolution, designed for this purpose.

Speak the Language

Fluency in the local language is obviously a crucial advantage, but people are of different minds about whether or not it is a necessity. Some contend that a director can function adequately with a full-time interpreter and local professional staff, others argue that it is inefficient to be reliant on a second full-time person, who ends up knowing everything that the director knows.

Certainly some directors who arrived "cold," with no experience with the USSR or Eastern Bloc, have adapted quickly and successfully, thanks to personal skills and a genuine curiosity toward the people and place. Others have met with disaster, or at best, found themselves in a cocoon apart from much of what goes on in daily life.

CHAPTER THREE

MAJOR NEEDS OF THE LOCAL NGO SECTOR

From Isolation to Organization

On an overcast day in October 1991, two months after the failure of communist hardliners to depose Mikhail Gorbachev, about a dozen people bearing the attire of village life sat at rows of tables in a small building on the grounds of the white Russian parliament building, scribbling on sheets of paper. They were writing to "that parliament building" across the driveway, begging for an audience with someone who might possibly help them with their personal problems.

One woman raised her sheaf of handwritten pages, interspersed with sheets of balding carbon paper, to display the terrible story of her daughter who had hearing problems and needed an operation. The mother had come all the way from the capital of Belarus to plead with the Russian parliament to intervene and provide the financial subsidy to get her daughter the treatment she needed.

Scenes of such lonely appeals for help direct from the state were a common feature of the Soviet landscape, and can still be witnessed today. But to a visitor returning to Russia, startling developments have taken place. Thousands of people like the Belarusian mother have banded together with others and formed somewhere around a quarter of a million grassroots organizations across the former Soviet Union.

Precise figures on the number of local NGOs are impossible to gather, for only a small portion of them officially register. Some avoid registration because it is still a long and confounding process; outside of Moscow and other major cities it can be difficult for a fledgling organization to get hold of information on the registration process itself. Others choose not to register if they are small and poorly financed, because they feel they could not afford to operate if they were forced to meet the requirements of the tax auditors. Finally, accurate figures are elusive, as registry lists are always changing.

Most striking is the level of experience and sophistication already achieved by some of the NGOs, which prompted an NGO expert returning—with skepticism—after a two-year absence to remark at the "astonishing changes" she had not expected. She had come across local NGOs that were so sophisticated, they could function just about anywhere in the world.

Accompanying these sharp advances in expertise and sophistication is a dramatic increase in the availability the office tools they need to "function anywhere in the world." Until five years ago, access to offices with phones and electric typewriters—not to mention fax machines, photocopiers, and computers—was severely limited. Indeed, such facilities were rare in general, and seen only at the highest rung of officialdom, or in the directors' suites of elite institutes and factories. The infusion of international aid, which from the United States reached nearly $2.5 billion in 1994 (almost half to Russia) has given many groups a great boost. Under the auspices of USAID, the European Community's TACIS program, and several foundations, local NGOs have established clearinghouses and support centers in various regions of Russia, and more recently in the Caucasus and Central Asia.

Other groups commission local researchers to survey the needs of regions, and publish regular magazines and newsletters on the work of the NGO sector. These and some gradual efforts at self-sustaining fundraising, demonstrate that a number of local groups are no longer cut off from communications and information.

All this is taking place in the *terra incognita* of post-Soviet legislation—new constitutions, civil and commercial codes; laws on refugees and migrants. As listed in Appendix V, nearly 70 pieces of legislation are known to exist (others are being drafted), on matters of public associations, foundations and tax codes. An aggressive, if stormy, collaboration by a number of Russian NGOs, finally thrashed out legislation on non-profit organizations, which became law in the spring of 1995. In several other republics, the legislative process is grinding on as well, but results vary significantly in content and consistency of implementation.

Regrettably, the field of forced migration is relatively underdeveloped as an NGO endeavor, although there are individuals and organizations working in related areas of human rights monitoring, advocacy, and legal counseling who are approaching high levels of professionalism.

From Organizing to Networking

As a number of the older NGOs in Moscow expanded their work in the early 1990s and international NGOs streamed in on the wave of Western funding, a regular roundtable discussion was established under the auspices of the MacArthur Foundation. The need for a forum in which to exchange information, let alone try to coordinate work efforts, was something utterly new for the local and international NGOs operating in the capital. Before long, the head of one of the leading Russian groups announced that the local NGOs wanted to conduct their own roundtable, to be able to concentrate on the issues more specific to their needs. It was a breakthrough for the Russian NGOs to meet locally and share information. Recently the leaders of at least two important groups have begun to collaborate in training and fundraising activities.

While the Western aid for "democracy-building" has stressed cooperation among local NGOs, it has been a rough-and-tumble process, and international NGOs working closely with the local sector say that time is required for the institutions to build themselves up to the level that they actually share program interests. These efforts can be undermined by sometimes-divisive competition and rivalry, as the outside sources of funding are dramatically slashed.

Moscow vs. Periphery

Donors should be cautioned that Moscow's NGO sector is not typical of the rest of the ex-USSR, nor even faintly replicated in most areas of Russia itself. One should be prepared for everything from scenes such as the Belarusian mother with her carbon paper, to outright government bans, detention, and beatings of NGO activists in some of the republics of Central Asia.

This contrast reflects the legacy of centralization from the Soviet era, compounded by the inclination of Western donors to link with groups in the capital. One international NGO discovered a community north of the Arctic Circle where people were trying to organize a non-profit group, but they had never heard the term "third sector"—a phrase commonly used among Moscow's NGOs for voluntary agencies.

The contrast between the dynamic, even adventuresome NGO sector in Moscow, and the rest of Russia also mirrors the progression of politics in the republic, where Moscow has been the hub of much of the organized democratic activism. So removed are

Muscovites from the more conservative provinces that they were simply stunned in 1993 when the flamboyant nationalist Vladimir Zhirinovsky won a huge vote in the parliamentary elections.

Over the years, international NGO officials invited to conduct organizational training seminars across Russia, have encountered the same "political gap" in the views of local NGOs. The following anecdote capsulizes this discovery, recounted by an international trainer who has travelled to many communities in the Russian Federation to offer seminars in civic participation to local NGOs seeking it. It begins with a favorite joke she regularly used to break the ice with a new group:

A black Volga sedan full of old politburo guys pulls out of the Kremlin gate and they see a little boy standing with a box of tiny newborn puppies. He's made a sign that reads: "Soviet puppies for sale." The Politburo bosses are delighted, and stop the car to get out and praise the little boy.

"How patriotic you are, what a good socialist!" they say. Two weeks later, the same group of Politburo members drives out of the Kremlin and sees the same little boy with the same box of puppies. But this time his sign shows the word "Soviet" crossed out, and the words written, "democratic" puppies for sale.

"What's this!" the Politburo bosses shout, and the driver screeches to a halt. They get out and demand to know, "What's going on here? What is meant by this? Are you a traitor to socialism? Why did you change from Soviet to democratic puppies for sale?"

The boy looks up at the bosses and replies, "Well, they've opened their eyes."

As the trainer recalls, when she told this joke, most groups "laughed their heads off. But one day I went to a training session out in a conservative town on the Volga River and walked into the room, only to see the whole front row seated with very old men with their chests covered with veterans medals. 'Oops,' I thought. I don't think that joke will be the best one to break the ice out here."

The political gulf can also appear greater than it actually is. The same trainer recalls holding seminars with NGO leaders who described themselves as staunch communists, who had no use for the "new democrats." But once they opened a discussion about the specifics of their own NGO activities, they often described pursuits that sounded rather "democratic"—such as lobbying the city and county councils on behalf of disabled people; spreading public information about the problems facing people with disabilities; pushing to adapt facilities for wheelchair access—in short, doing advocacy for these people. But as soon as the NGO trainer asked whether the local group was involved in "democratic activities," their instant retort was, "Absolutely not!"

It comes as no surprise that a 1995 survey of the charitable causes supported by non-governmental groups in the provinces revealed that the issue of "human rights" was a concept that enjoyed virtually no comprehension or importance. According to Charities Aid Foundation (CAF), which commissioned the study, compared with the grinding reality of daily life, issues such as civil and political rights were found to be unimportant—despite the attention given to them in the media.[2]

The findings of the CAF research have been mirrored by the experience of an NGO support center in Siberia, which initiated a series of meetings geared to building group relations. The subjects offered were education, environment, social services, cultural activities, and human rights. The session that drew the best-attendance was social services; the worst-attended session covered human rights.

Searching for the issues that do concern communities in Russia, Charities Aid surveyed 157 non-commercial institutions in five regions of Russia from 1994 to 1995, and found that the majority of these non-profit organizations focused on the problems of handicapped people and low-income families. [5] As for the Russian population-at-large, CAF conducted another survey of 1007 people in Moscow and its surrounding region, on public attitudes toward charity and donation. To the query concerning which issues they support in principle, but do not actually contribute money or voluntary time to, there were four leading responses: protection of animals, people with disabilities, the elderly, and the environment. [6]

Classifying NGOs and Their Needs

Western experts working with the non-profit sector in the ex-USSR, repeatedly observe that in the hierarchy of local organizations, those based in Moscow tend to be the most sophisticated, and so much so that they may resist any suggestion of training. Even some which function very well and with professionalism may not believe that there is a need to take the additional steps to create a real structure for the organization to survive and grow over the long term. At the other extreme, there are regions beyond the capital where people have never had experience drafting a budget or a work plan, and needless to say, have never worked with up-to-date computer packages designed for financial management.

In an attempt to put some order to the jumble of local NGOs, it is useful to consider the hierarchy suggested by a staff member of one international NGO with extensive work in the former Soviet republics. [7] He loosely classifies groups in four categories according to criteria reflecting their levels of development: advanced, intermediate, beginning, and potential. Whether advanced or potential, all local NGOs require some kind of training, and many believe that it is most effective to foster local groups to conduct the actual seminars. Material can be supplied from outside sources, adapted and translated; but the first step should be to identify a local group with training skills or interest, and elaborate on it.

Local NGOs falling into the advanced category are viewed to be sufficiently established and structured as an organization to endure for some time. As would be the case at international organizations, advanced NGOs have full-time staff, workplans, and financial plans, and are active fundraisers. They also play a role in making government policy.

NGOs that have reached an intermediate level also have mission statements and full-time staff, and appreciate the need for management structures. Their notable limitations are in the lack of formal annual budgets and workplans, and therefore they tend to acquire funds by the project, rather than by an overall organizational program.

Beginning NGOs can be the most exciting to work with in certain ways, because of their initiative, ideas and enthusiastic volunteers. But while some of them have defined their mission, their potential to develop into an enduring entity may be hampered by not recognizing the need for building an organizational structure. Despite the fact that some beginning organizations may carry out successful projects, they lack secure funding sources and their financing is sporadic.

There must be thousands of potential NGOs out there, registered or not, groups of people working together in a shared interest. What they lack in organizational structure and project completion, they make up for in enthusiasm, and may possess some promising attributes to foster.

Consistent with their varying levels of accomplishment, the

needs of the NGO categories differ as well. All of them need assistance with funding, but the advanced and intermediate levels specifically need help finding international sources and international NGOs interested in partnerships. Both levels also can benefit from organizational consulting experts who can address the problems special to each group; and both also need help in establishing contact with local government and businesses, to encourage working relationships and philanthropic giving.

While the advanced and intermediates have already established many of their organizational strengths, beginners and potentials need a great deal of information and training on basic organizational issues. They also need funding for specific projects, which in carrying them out, helps to develop the organization itself. Beginners would benefit from association with organizations that are stronger than theirs, whereas the potential NGOs would benefit from focussed discussions about drafting an organizational charter and proposals for fundraising.

Substantive Areas of Need
Where NGOs Can Make an Impact

To discover the substantive areas of need in the former Soviet Union, it is not necessary to voyage to the remote reaches of the once-forbidden frontiers. Anyone who has travelled through villages in central and southern Russia can immediately see the dearth of services in health care and education, much less forced migration and human rights.

If such is the landscape in Russia, the pattern is often more pronounced the further one ventures beyond some borders of the Russian Federation. As Moscow's economic ties dissolved and subsidies disappeared, these republics saw the collapse of their economies and service sectors, and received only a fraction of the international investment and NGO support that poured into Moscow during the early 1990s. Their predicament has been compounded by bloody conflicts which have wracked Azerbaijan, Armenia, Georgia, Moldova, Tajikistan and southern Russia, hastening the breakdown of law and order, and in some instances, reducing the native population's pursuits to the grinding drive for sheer survival. Needless to say, the pressures on displaced populations are even worse, and the following needs sorely apply to them.

Human Rights

Far from the idealistic hopes held in some international circles that the collapse of the Communist regime would diminish human rights abuses in the former Soviet Union, the need is greater than ever to support local organizations monitoring the wide range of problems that have arisen with the increase in physical mobility and political expression.

In Russia, local human rights monitors are swamped with reporting violations against the civilian population in the war against Chechnya, and the arbitrary expulsions of ethnic Caucasians, identified by their darker skin color, by the Moscow authorities. The resignation of Russia's exasperated human rights commissioner is a recent indication of work that still remains to be done to monitor and prevent abuses of international human rights, refugee and humanitarian law.

There is also a great need to support volunteer lawyers who currently staff the weekly legal clinic for forced migrants in Moscow and two provincial cities. Most of the republics report the need for affordable legal counsel to refugees and internally displaced persons (IDPs), who seek help with registration of status, jobs, housing, and compensation for their losses.

NGOs in the Baltic states need support for monitoring of their own restrictive citizenship laws, which affect the rights of resident Russians, and for advocating more humane treatment of the small trickle of asylum seekers, mainly from Africa and the Near East, who are summarily detained. None of the Baltic States has acceded to the international refugees treaties.

In other republics, further from the international eye, detentions and intimidation have continued apace, effectively immobilizing many of the most active community leaders who would form the backbone of an NGO sector. State repression tends to be less harsh on community groups dedicated to cultural affairs or assistance to the disabled. But then those organizations in the former republics are hampered by the lack of funds to rent even the most modest office space, pay for a telephone, and set up the most basic office equipment.

Legal System

Despite the progress made by some of the republics in drafting new constitutions, endorsing international conventions, and developing laws dealing with forced migration, the fair and consistent application of these instruments seems to be a long way off. In general, where there are laws, the administrative procedures to implement them are lacking. Where there are administrative procedures for implementation, they are often not followed. In any case, no state allocates sufficient funds to meet its obligations to refugees or displaced persons under the law.

Russian NGOs have made great strides in influencing legislative enactments, such as the law on non-profit associations, but still need assistance to press ahead with more equitable tax laws, as well as reform of legislation on refugees and asylum. The same can be said in the extreme for most of the other Soviet republics. And in Turkmenistan, Uzbekistan and Tajikistan, for the moment, local NGOs seeking to create a more just legal system are seriously hindered by inadequacies in the rule of law (see Appendix IV).

Education

One of the cruelest legacies of the Soviet Union is the empty coffer left for basic education. Throughout the republics, public schools lack basic supplies, let alone modern materials and textbooks introducing new concepts such as diversity and tolerance. Again, the situation is very uneven. The rise of a private education sector has siphoned off many of the most skilled teachers to expensive, well-equipped *gymnasia,* while children in the same town may be reading history books written by the Soviet-era ministry. Often, principals have shown NGO-like initiative, and gone out to their local industrial barons to raise money for their own schools.

Communications and Information

Not enough can be said about local NGOs' need for access to independent, reliable information about everything from their own specialty, to the daily news in their own republic and the world. All forms of assistance are deeply needed: funds to install a telephone line; telephones themselves; fax machines, personal computers and computer modems.

Health

In all the republics, health conditions are bordering on catastrophic for the native-born populations, and dislocated populations without proper documents can be at even greater risk. With sanitation and preventive health systems in disrepair, communicable diseases such as diphtheria and cholera have broken out at an alarming rate. Health maintenance is deplorable, environmentally-related illnesses are epidemic in some regions, and the average life expectancy has been declining.

Many cities and many more villages across the continent have no access to basic medicines, or else the medicine supply is controlled by local merchants who charge unaffordable prices for them. Poor people, further impoverished by the deregulation of prices in 1992 and the sharp rise in the cost of living, have nowhere to turn, and elderly persons in this category are the most vulnerable.

Another health problem afflicts people who have been uprooted by war and ethnic violence, i.e. the debilitating effect of post-traumatic stress. Several small steps have been taken by local non-governmental organizations with international assistance to treat some of the most acute cases in Georgia and Abkhazia. But future attempts at lasting reconciliation and stability in southern Russia, Azerbaijan, and Tajikistan may be impeded if this problem is not adequately addressed.

Organizational Training and Management

For the more advanced groups in the NGO sector, this is an ongoing need, and it is widely recommended for donors to support local NGO support centers and clearinghouses which have begun to establish their own training modules, keyed into the local realities.

Many people interviewed for this report expressed apprehension over the political uncertainty looming over Russia's imminent presidential election. There were voices of doom, fear and despair that a "change at the top" would spell the certain end of freedom. But there were equal numbers of voices arguing that the grassroots developments in ordinary life had driven an irreparable crack in the wall that once ensured totalitarian isolation.

Much of the work that may endure the test of political turmoil will likely be the most modest and least conspicuous—that of small community groups, gathering and distributing reliable information on nuclear safety, help for the disabled, or the rights of people different from themselves.

Georgian refugees fleeing conflict in Abkhazia.

CHAPTER FOUR

PROFILES OF THE REPUBLICS

ARMENIA

Capital: Yerevan
Total area: 29,800 sq. km.
Population: 3,557,284 (July 1995 est.)
Ethnic groups: Armenian 93%, Azeri 3%, Russian 2%, other
(mostly Yezidi Kurds) 2% (1989). As of the end of 1994, most
Azeris had emigrated from Armenia.
Religions: Armenian Orthodox 94%
Population growth rate: 0.94% (1995 est.)
Net migration rate: -6.68 migrants/1,000 population (1995 est.)
Refugees and asylum seekers: 295,800 (5,800 from Georgia)
Languages: Armenian 96%, Russian 2%, other 2%
GDP per capita: $2,290 (1994 estimate as extrapolated from
World Bank estimate for 1992)
Telephone system: 177 telephones/1,000 persons

Brief Context

Wedged between Georgia and Azerbaijan, which have each endured bloody battles over ancient disputed territories, Armenia itself has been engaged in an undeclared conflict with neighboring Azerbaijan since 1988, the longest-running war in the former Soviet Union. Fighting broke out in mountainous region of

Nagorno-Karabakh, located in Azerbaijan, when the ethnic Armenian majority declared its intention to be united with kindred Armenia. The violence stunned the two republics, whose Christian and Muslim nationals had mingled and intermarried for centuries. As many as a quarter of a million ethnic Armenians and Azeris each lived in the other republic.

In the tumult that followed, two brutal pogroms against Armenians living in Azerbaijan triggered mass reprisals. The result was an exodus of both ethnic groups from their opposing republics to titular homelands that many of them had never known. In all, 500,000 are believed to have been uprooted; some of the most educated among them have spent the subsequent years with uncertain status in Moscow.

Not only was Yerevan unprepared to accommodate the huge wave of skilled, urban Armenians leaving Azerbaijan in 1988, but its problems were compounded by the earthquake in Spitak in December 1988, which left tens of thousands dead or homeless.

The war, fought with weapons from the Soviet arsenal, was a seesaw affair for several years, with the sides gaining and losing ground from each other. As Azerbaijan's government foundered under the mounting criticism of its war defeats, Armenian forces pressed their stunning offensive in the Spring of 1993, capturing all the territory in and around the disputed mountain enclave. Azeris and Kurds living in those areas fled in panic, and languished through the scorching summer in temporary camps along the Iranian border with Azerbaijan.

The consequences of the war have been disastrous for both sides. Azerbaijan promptly cut its oil and gas lines to Armenia, choking its industry, transportation and electricity year after year, and plunging it into freezing winters without heat.

In the context of Armenia's many hardships, the needs of refugees and migrants have taken a lower priority to the general population's needs for energy, food, housing and work. Half of the country's industry has ground to a halt. Thousands of people are still living in temporary shelter erected after the earthquake of 1988 and tracts of land lie in rubble.

Non-Governmental Efforts

When the energy shortages reached a crisis during the particularly harsh winter of 1993, Armenia saw a great influx of international aid, and dozens of Western NGOs rushed to Yerevan to bring emergency assistance and assess the longer term needs. Few of these or local NGOs deal specifically with refugees and migration issues. Up to now, the Armenian refugees from Azerbaijan receive material assistance mainly from the State Committee on Refugees, International Organization for Migration (IOM) and United Nations High Commissioner for Refugees (UNHCR).

According to an Armenian who heads a local NGO, more than nine hundred NGOs are officially registered in the republic. Many of them are active in their delivery of services, but only a fraction could be considered at the "advanced" level. Relations with the government are "polite, but limited," primarily due to lack of interest from the government, which is preoccupied with other pressing concerns. This NGO official said that he and others in non-profit circles were hoping for more contact between authorities and the voluntary sector.

Armenia's local NGOs suffer from many of the same limitations that impede similar groups throughout the former Soviet Union: many have no office, no official address, no phone and no reliable means of communication. As a first step toward remedying this, an NGO support center has been set up in Yerevan by the Armenian Assemblies of America, where NGOs can come together and receive crucial training in organizational development. The NGO support center also encourages groups working in the field of conflict resolution and peace.

Legislation pertaining to the registration of public associations goes back to 1989. As of March 1996, a controversial new draft law was under debate in the parliament. A number of local NGOs have been actively lobbying the parliament to make the law more conducive to NGO development. As in other republics, Armenian tax law is a drain on the non-profit sector and the banking system is also an obstacle.

An issue mentioned by Armenians interviewed for this report was the untapped pool of human resources found among the 290,000 ethnic Armenians who fled Azerbaijan from 1988-onward. One estimate suggests that at least three-quarters of these refugees and returnees were trained as engineers, doctors and other professionals, but many have not found homes or employment in any city. An NGO expert in Yerevan pointed out that these refugees could be encouraged to form NGOs themselves, along the model of other associations already organized for the support of poor people.

Along with the need for refugee groups to become more active in NGO work, experts in Yerevan cited the need for legal services, to provide a range of consultations in matters pertaining to refugee resettlement and status. Again, there is no shortage of personnel for this; a lawyers association and a legal advisory center already exist, but it is extremely difficult to find lawyers who will work on a voluntary basis.

AZERBAIJAN

Capital: Baku (Baki)
Total area: 86,600 sq. km.
Population: 7,789,886 (July 1995 est.)
Ethnic groups: Azeri 90%, Dagestani Peoples 3.2%, Russian 2.5%,
Armenian 2.3%, other 2% (1995 est.). Most Armenians live in the
separatist Nagorno-Karabakh region.
Religions: Muslim 93.4%, Russian Orthodox 2.5%, Armenian
Orthodox 2.3%, other 1.8% (1995 est.)
Population growth rate: 1.32% (1995 est.)
Net migration rate: -2.32 migrants/per1,000 (1995 est.)
Refugees and asylum seekers: 279,000 (50,000 from Uzbekistan)
Internally displaced persons: 630,000
Languages: Azeri 89%, Russian 3%, Armenian 2%,
other 6% (1995 est.)
GDP per capita: $1,790 (1994 estimate as extrapolated from World
Bank estimate for 1992)
Telephone system: 90 telephones/1,000 persons (1991)

Brief Context

Since January 1990, when the Soviet Army cracked down on national demonstrators in Baku, Azerbaijan has lurched from coups and elections, to attempted overthrows, often triggered by its overwhelming defeats by Armenian forces fighting for control of Nagorno-Karabakh. The combat largely ended in mid-1993, following the decisive offensive by Armenian forces, which took control over a fifth of Azerbaijan. Hundreds of thousands of Azeris and Kurds fled from their towns and villages surrounding the mountain region of Nagorno-Karabakh. Some settled in emergency camps and others in public buildings.

Altogether, as many as 630,000 people have been uprooted by

this war, and according to Azeri human rights monitors, the critical shortage of temporary housing for these people continues. The permanent solution of returning to their homes has been clouded by the fact that many of the houses that were not destroyed have reportedly been occupied by others after they fled.

In addition to these IDPs, who constitute a portion of the 900,000-1.1 million people displaced on Azerbaijani soil, the Baku government has been host to roughly 100,000 Muslim people known as "Meskhetian Turks," one of the national minorities among the "punished peoples" deported by the Stalin during the 1940s. Loaded onto freight cars in their native region of southern Georgia in November 1944, the Meskhetians endured a harrowing journey to Uzbekistan, where they were deposited in the fertile Fergana Valley and lived for more than 40 years.

In 1989, the Meskhetians had the terrible fate of being deported a second time, in the wake of violent riots against them by neighboring Uzbeks. Initially evacuated to Russia, many have gradually drifted southward to Azerbaijan. From there, they have sought approval from the Georgian government to return to their native territory. But local opposition to the Meskhetians in their former homeland has not given hope for a speedy repatriation, and some reports estimate that as many as 70 percent have found jobs and integrated into Azerbaijan.

Non-Governmental Efforts

Following the acceleration of fighting and population displacement in 1993, Azerbaijan has seen an influx of aid from the international relief community, but it has been severely limited by the U.S. Freedom Support Act of 1992. Section 907, passed in 1994, prohibits most aid to Azerbaijan because of the blockade it has imposed on Armenia, making it the only former Soviet republic barred from receiving U.S. aid.

American NGOs with experience in Azerbaijan have sharply criticized Section 907 for its terrible impact on the relief assistance desperately needed by the masses of refugees and IDPs. In spite of the legislation, a number of American NGOs have tried to find limited ways to work within its constraints. A range of UN agencies, along with the ICRC, are also operating in Azerbaijan. Although the emergency phase ended some time ago, a large number of IDPs still require assistance, and the work of humanitarian organizations remains necessary.

Faced with the long-term needs of the displaced population and the absence of change in the political situation for nearly two years, some international NGOs have expressed a desire to hand over more responsibility to local NGOs for the delivery of assistance. But most of Azerbaijan's local NGOs are new and inexperienced, and it has been difficult to find local groups that are sufficiently developed to handle the level of operation required.

As throughout the ex-USSR, Azerbaijan is feeling the effects of the highly bureaucratic and regimented Soviet educational system, which rarely fostered the skills required to work independently, efficiently, and creatively. Therefore one of the largest unmet needs cited by international NGO officials working in Baku is the improvement of financial management, program development and basic skills in personnel and time management.

Illustrating the disparity in figures pertaining to NGO registration, recent reports put a total of 192,000 on paper, but some local experts suggest that less than half of them are "real." Very few, in any case, deal specifically with the issues of IDPs. One Azeri NGO representative interviewed for this book points out that the phenomenon of GONGOs, so familiar several years ago in Russia, has caught up with Azerbaijan, and warns that some are trying to conduct parallel work to the *bona fide* local groups.

An NGO support center has been slower in emerging in

Azerbaijan, although international NGOs such as ISAR, a predominantly environmental organization, are broadening their focus to work on developing the fledgling NGO sector in general. International NGOs working in Azerbaijan report that the government has been generally supportive of their work; it does not, for the most part, intervene in the management of the relief assistance, and even makes an effort to facilitate it.

One of the daily challenges to working in Azerbaijan, nevertheless, is dealing with the bureaucracy, which runs the gamut from getting registered and processing goods through customs, to obtaining an automobile license plate. Most issues can be resolved successfully, but often require a great deal of time and energy.

As one NGO representative in Baku describes it, Azerbaijan is "still trying to figure out how to run itself." Communication and coordination between government departments is scarce, as is coordination among the different levels of government. Taxes, on the other hand, appear to be a source of good news in Azerbaijan, as the staff of international NGOs are exempt from income tax—levied at 40 percent or more.

The banking system is described by an international official in Baku as "somewhat chaotic." The rules for banking change on a regular basis, not only as a result of the frequent changes in government, but also as a function of "unofficial" fees charged by government or banking personnel for their own interest.

One must be braced for rules that change from day-to-day concerning bank transfers involving dollar or local currency accounts, as well as new surcharges applied arbitrarily. Still, the banking system works sufficiently to be able to avoid the extremely high risk of dealing only in enormous sums of cash. Theft tends to be measured in terms of "skimming" by local staff, and blatant theft has been rarer than in neighboring Georgia or southern Russia. In Baku, the main threat to security is the occasional coup attempt, which occurs rarely, and is usually quickly contained. Among field staff, the greatest security risks would occur in the event of renewed fighting. But a cease-fire has been in effect since May 1994.

As for violent crime, an international NGO representative in Baku describes it as "almost non-existent"—in sharp contrast with other countries in the fSU. Many attribute this to the traditions and Muslim culture of Azerbaijan, but with the continuing decline in the standard of living, the relative civility could change.

Finding qualified Azeris to work in the NGO sector would not be so difficult if not for the stiff competition with the foreign oil companies in Baku, whose salaries and greater job security are understandably alluring. In Baku more than other capitals, international NGOs must be prepared for the possibility of investing time training in new local staff, only to find them poached by foreign oil companies.

As in Armenia, Azerbaijan has a pool of largely untapped skills among the IDPs from the war zone, exemplified by one new NGO in the Sabirabad IDP Camp, which has been cited for its work in the psychological rehabilitation of children in that camp. Funded initially by the Norwegian Refugee Council, "Buta" (Children's Humanitarian Foundation) began working with a target population of roughly 2000 IDP children, using sports and creative arts, and especially exploring role-play for conflict resolution and prevention.

Once again, local NGO representatives underscore the need for legal services in Azerbaijan, especially for the IDPs still living in tent camps. The Azerbaijan Center for Human Rights, a local NGO which monitors human rights problems, is seeking to publish a newspaper for IDPs and refugees to provide information on local laws, human rights, and international policy.

BELARUS

Capital: Minsk
Total area: 207,600 sq. km.
Population: 10,437,418 (July 1995 est.)
Ethnic groups: Belarusian 77.9%, Russian 13.2%, Polish 4.1%,
Ukrainian 2.9%, other 1.9%
Religions: Eastern Orthodox, other
Population growth rate: 0.3% (1995 est.)
Net migration rate: 1.27 migrants/ per 1,000 population (1995 est.)
Refugees and asylum seekers: 18,800
Languages: Belarusian, Russian, other
GDP per capita: $5,130 (1994 estimate as extrapolated from World
Bank estimate for 1992)
Telephone system: 180 telephones/1,000 persons (1992)

Brief Context

Belarus may have been spared the ethnic conflict that has
uprooted hundreds of thousands in Armenia and Azerbaijan in
the wake of the Soviet Union's collapse, but its land and people
have been ravaged by the wars and invasions that have torn
through this great plain bridging Europe and Russia. World War
II alone claimed the lives of a quarter of the population, and the
capital Minsk was left in rubble.

The majority of Belarus' displaced population today have been
uprooted by a more recent man-made disaster: the 1986 accident
at the nuclear reactor in Chernobyl, Ukraine. Consistent with
Belarus' history in the shadow of greater neighbors, the tragedy it
suffered from Chernobyl was eclipsed by the concern for the
immediate victims in Ukraine. But scientists estimate that roughly 70 percent of the fallout was deposited on Belarus, and two-
thirds of Belarus' best arable land was rendered unusable by

radioactive contamination. Thousands were forced to abandon their towns and villages.

Now, a decade later, thyroid cancer in children has appeared at an alarming rate, and the psychological stress of living with the radioactive danger has taken a toll on the population. The President of Belarus recently told a conference of nuclear experts in Vienna that 25 percent of his annual budget went to dealing with the effects of the catastrophe.

Far from keeping pace with the economic reforms in Russia, Belarus has lagged behind, following a path as conservative politically as economically. Change has been extremely slow, and visitors often remark how much life still resembles the Soviet Union. Funds for fuel and raw materials are scarce, and, as elsewhere in the former USSR, many workers go months without wages. Medical supplies are lacking at affordable prices.

Non-Governmental Efforts

As the state fails to provide for the vast needs in social services, an enormous challenge faces the more than 700 NGOs that have registered thus far. But reflecting the isolation of Belarus in general, its newly evolving NGO sector suffers from a dearth of information and resources. Without a visible humanitarian emergency, it has attracted very few international agencies or NGOs, and most of the major Western donors—the European Community, the United States, and leading foundations—send their regional representatives for periodic visits.

To begin to remedy this, United Way Belarus has operated an NGO Development Center in Minsk since 1995. Staffed by Belarusians, and assisted by an American consultant and a volunteer board of Minsk community leaders, the center provides a wide range of technical assistance and services. These include legal advice on legislation and banking; seminars on fundraising, strategic planning, accounting and taxation; and information on project development and grant-writing.

The NGO center also sponsors a variety of monthly meetings to stimulate the sharing of information among local NGOs, and offers registered NGOs access to its library, computers, printers, photocopier, fax, phones and e-mail. For local NGOs far from the capital, there are plans to open affiliate offices in the cities of Brest, Vitebsk, and Gomel.

But the tightening of government control over civic organizations—suspending independent trade unions last year and barring publication of some liberal newspapers—has hindered NGOs as well. International human rights monitors report that an order issued by the government has required all local NGOs to re-register, and to date, as many as half—including the Belarusian Bureau on Human Rights—have reportedly not been reinstated.

One NGO representative in Minsk explains that there is a great deal of official mistrust of NGOs, more than in many of the former republics. Many people in the general population also suspect that NGOs are really commercial companies pretending to be humanitarian organizations.

To dispel these notions, one of the main goals of the NGO Center is to stimulate public education, and to inform the President's Administration on the role the non-governmental sector can play. It is also striving to provide input into proposed national legislation that would affect the activities of NGOs.

GEORGIA

Capital: Tbilisi
Total area: 69,700 sq. km.
Population: 5,725,972 (July 1995 est.)
Ethnic groups: Georgian 70.1%, Armenian 8.1%, Russian 6.3%,
Azeri 5.7%, Ossetian 3%, Abkhaz 1.8%, other 5%
Religions: Georgian Orthodox 65%, Russian Orthodox 10%,
Muslim 11%, Armenian Orthodox 8%, unknown 6%
Population growth rate: 0.77% (1995 est.)
Net migration rate: 0.66 migrants/1,000 population (1995 est.)
Internally displaced persons: 260,000
Languages: Georgian 71% (official), Armenian 7%, Azeri 6%,
Russian 9%, other 7%
GDP per capita: $1,060 (1994 estimate as extrapolated from World
Bank estimate for 1992)
Telephone system: 117 telephones/1,000 persons (1993)

Brief Context

After three years of armed conflict, rampant lawlessness and economic collapse, the caucasian republic of Georgia greeted 1996 in a state of relative calm; but the problem of internally displaced people smoldered on. Neither of Georgia's two regional conflicts—with the mountainous area of South Ossetia and with the Black Sea region of Abkhazia—has been fully resolved. This is so despite the efforts of the Organization for Security and Cooperation in Europe (OSCE) in the South Ossetian dispute, and UN-sponsored negotiations and a Russian peacekeeping force in Abkhazia.

Across Western Georgia and throughout Tbilisi, schools, resorts, tourist hotels and many other public buildings are bursting with a quarter-million ethnic Georgians displaced from these areas. The many who have survived off local and family traditions of hospitality have drained their hosts of all their reserves.

Though tens of thousands of IDPs have spontaneously returned to their homes in certain parts of Abkhazia (estimates range from 20,000-50,000), a repatriation program organized by the UNHCR in 1994 failed to guarantee the protection needed for the vast majority of ethnic Georgians to go back permanently.

Like Armenia, Georgia has suffered severe fuel shortages for several years, and industry has ground to a virtual halt. This, and the miserable standard of living, have driven a number of ethnic Russians to leave the country.

Non-Governmental Efforts

With the return of Eduard Shevardnadze to Georgia in March 1992, many expected his international renown to bring the republic a flood of Western support. But a significant increase in humanitarian aid and international NGO activity began the following year, as the Georgian army retreated from Abkhazia and thousands of ethnic Georgian civilians took flight in their shirtsleeves over the snow-covered mountains. By the close of 1993, most of the UN agencies and leading international NGOs concerned with emergency relief were operating in Georgia, and dozens of local NGOs stepped up their work.

It was rough going for many of the international groups initially working in Western Georgia, whose cars were hijacked or blown up over land-mines. Offices were raided and robbed at gunpoint. Government officials often shrugged and said there was little they could do to control the crime, particularly as the suspected perpetrators were often linked to a paramilitary group close to the government.

To make matters worse, the banking sector was ill-equipped to handle the large currency transfers for international NGOs, so they increased their risks by having to conduct their relief work with great quantities of cash.

While some NGOs report that they have successfully wired money for the past two years, others still regard the banking system is still a problem, as are the tax laws. But according to international officials in Tbilisi, the tax system is being examined in a joint effort by the international aid community, a local NGO called GYLA (Georgia Young Lawyers Association), and another group recently established to offer advice to local and international community.

Overall, the daily atmosphere in Georgia has changed markedly, especially since the sweeping arrests in late 1995 of the paramilitary gangs who instigated much of the crime that brought Georgia to its knees. One NGO official working in Tbilisi says that governmental officials ranging from ministers to parliamentarians have officially expressed positive views toward working with Georgian NGOs. Legislation relevant to non-profit organizations is under review, with input from some local NGOs; there are hopes for a law which is supportive of non-governmental groups to be enacted soon.

During 1995, a number of local NGOs took part in training programs offered by United Nations agencies (UN Volunteers, Department of Humanitarian Affairs, UNHCR), ISAR, and others. Sessions focused on how to form, manage and find funding for a local NGO. Georgia's non-profit sector engages in a wide range of interests, and several groups, such as the lawyers association GYLA, are cited as fairly advanced organizations.

Support centers now offer a great deal of information to Georgian NGOs, through the International Telecommunications and Information Center, with reference library, and ISAR. Together these two NGOs sponsor the monthly newsletter *New*

Georgia, which provides of information on funding sources, international study opportunities, and local seminars in NGO management and development.

The bitterness left by the ethnic clashes in Abkhazia and Ossetia is an issue that has only barely been addressed. In early 1995, the UN Volunteers (UNV) conducted workshops with a number of local NGOs concerned with efforts at peace and conflict resolution. With UNICEF, UNV has supported the publication of a children's magazine to raise awareness of the importance of peace and conflict prevention.

As in most other republics, a leading obstacle facing NGO development is the lack of funds. Local and international telephone lines are another great impediment for everyone needing to be in touch with places outside Georgia, and electronic mail is still not completely reliable.

KAZAKHSTAN

Capital: Almaty
Total area: 2,717,300 sq. km.
Population: 17,376,615 (July 1995 est.)
Ethnic groups: Kazakh 41.9%, Russian 37%, Ukrainian 5.2%,
German 4.7%, Uzbek 2.1%, Tatar 2%, other 7.1%
(1991 official data)
Religions: Muslim 47%, Russian Orthodox 44%,
Protestant 2%, other 7%
Population growth rate: 0.62% (1995 est.)
Net migration rate: -5.11 migrants/1,000 population (1995 est.)
Refugees and asylum seekers: 300
Languages: Kazakh (official language) spoken by over 40% of popu-
lation, Russian (language of inter-ethnic communication) spoken by
two-thirds of population and used in everyday business
GDP per capita: $3,200 (1994 estimate as extrapolated from World
Bank estimate for 1992)
Telephone system: 170 telephones/1000 persons in urban areas and
76 telephones/1000 persons in rural areas

Brief Context

A vast land, sweeping across the steppe which bridges Russia and Asia, the republic of Kazakhstan is coping with several migration problems, most pressing of which is the exodus of ethnic Russians and Germans.

The latter, long-time residents of the Volga region who were deported to Central Asia during World War II, are leaving in earnest, taking up Germany's offer to resettle them. As many as half a million Germans are estimated to have left since 1992, and one survey of the remaining 500,000 suggests that 65 percent of them also intend to leave.

Combined with the ethnic Russians, a total of well over a million people have left Kazakhstan since the demise of the USSR, and with them went a sizeable proportion of the republic's skilled labor and technical force. Although the Kazakh government has urged them to stay, the steady decline in living standards is driving them to seek work in other countries.

While Kazakhstan's leading ethnic minorities shrink, the government in Almaty has invited some 30,000 ethnic Kazakhs from Mongolia to immigrate, reportedly in order to increase the proportion of the titular nationality who are nearly outnumbered by ethnic Russians in their own country.

Roughly 140,000 ethnic Kazakhs altogether have immigrated since 1991, according to government sources, including from Iran and Turkey. Recently, the influx of Kazakhs has dwindled to a few thousand, perhaps due to the lack of material support promised by the government. Local human rights monitors have reports of ethnic Kazakhs leaving Kazakhstan to go back to their original homes.

Another immigration trend to emerge since the end of 1994 is the arrival of ethnic Chechens fleeing the heavy military assault by the Russian army. Kazakhstan was home to tens of thousands of Chechens and other ethnic groups from the Caucasus, who, as "punished peoples," were violently uprooted during the winter of 1943-44, and shipped in freight trains to the steppe lands. After terrible loss of life and thirteen years in exile the Chechens were permitted to return home. Many found their houses occupied or destroyed, and faced further discrimination by the Russian administration.

Less than four decades later, the Chechens were again uprooted when the Russian army bombarded and shelled their capital Grozny and many villages and towns, in an attempt to crush the independence-minded government. Of the hundreds of thousands who fled the onslaught that began in December 1994, some 10,000 Chechens returned to the land of their former deportation, seeking shelter with families who had remained behind in Almaty and the southern region of the republic.

The war and upheaval in Tajikistan, to the south, has also produced several thousand refugees seeking safety in Kazakhstan. Those who were ethnic Kazakhs reportedly found shelter with extended families. Local human rights monitors say that the number of Tajiks is unknown, but most of them have found no homes or work; some have been seen begging in the streets.

Internal migration is posing an additional challenge to this Central Asian republic, as unemployed workers from the south head north to the regions being abandoned by the Russians and Germans. Other internal migrants are leaving the poor rural areas for the cities, also in search of work, but without residence permits. These patterns, according to local human rights monitors, are very scattered and difficult to monitor. Some of the recent urban migrants manage to find temporary work, but many seem to fall into the criminal world.

Non-Governmental Efforts

Regarded as a boom town to many foreign investors who have flocked to Kazakhstan for a stake in its energy reserves and trade opportunities, the largest Central Asian republic has only seen the gradual emergence of a non-governmental sector. Issues pertaining to forced migration and human rights have been addressed by the long-established Almaty Helsinki Group, which has played an active role in advocacy and legislative lobbying during the last few years.

NGOs connected with the independent trade union movement have also been active, if at times in confrontation with the government. But certain international NGO officials with experience in Kazakhstan are quick to stress that all local groups must exercise extreme caution in their work, as they live in the shadow of a highly centralized government which brooks little opposition.

Until recently, local NGOs tended to work on their own, with the Germans, for example, concentrating on their emigration problems, and others on theirs. But recently a local NGO support center has opened, called CASDIN (Central Asian Sustainable Development Information Network), staffed by Kazakhs, and assisting local groups with a newsletter and organizational advice.

Kazakhstan has an elaborate set of laws pertaining to public associations, and this spring its parliament has adopted a new law defining their rights and permitted activities. But in the field of forced migration, human rights monitors note that Kazakhstan has only adopted a law pertinent to the immigration of the Kazakhs from Mongolia. It has no general law on refugees, which poses a problem for the recently arrived Chechens, who gave up their residence status in Kazakhstan when they returned to Chechnya, and now find themselves with no legal status as refugees.

KYRGYZSTAN

Capital: Bishkek

Total area: 198,500 sq. km.

Population: 4,769,877 (July 1995 est.)

Ethnic groups: Kyrgyz 52.4%, Russian 21.5%, Uzbek 12.9%,
Ukrainian 2.5%, German 2.4%, other 8.3%

Religions: Muslim 47%, Russian Orthodox 44%,
Protestant 2%, other 7%

Population growth rate: 1.5% (1995 est.)

Net migration rate: -3.66 migrants/1,000 population (1995 est.)

Refugees and asylum seekers: 350

Languages: Kyrgyz (official language), Russian widely used

GDP per capita: $1,790 (1994 estimate as extrapolated from
World Bank estimate for 1992)

Telephone system: 76 telephones/1000 persons (December 1991)

Brief Context

Idealized by some as the Switzerland of Central Asia, and praised in the West for its comparatively smooth transition from Soviet rule, Kyrgyzstan has seen an exodus of ethnic Russians seeking a more secure future. Half a million have emigrated to other countries since 1989. In 1990, brief, but vicious, ethnic clashes broke out between Kyrgyz and local Uzbeks in the ancient Muslim pilgrimage city of Osh. The fights lasted for ten days, and in the wave of nationalist fervor that followed, many Russians left the country in fear.

Since then, human rights experts report that some 30 percent of the Russians who emigrated are trying to return but are unable to reclaim their Kyrgyz citizenship. The root of this problem goes back several years, to a law on foreigners passed under pressure from nationalist quarters, seeking to prevent the fleeing Russians from returning. A subsequent law on citizenship was less restrictive, but the issue is one of concern to groups working in forced migration.

Like most other Soviet republics, Kyrgyzstan is home to several ethnic minorities from other parts of the former Soviet Union; until the recent emigrations, Kyrgyz nationals accounted for less than 50 percent of the republic's population, with Uzbeks and Russians accounting for most of the remainder.

Non-Governmental Efforts

Given its relative stability through the last few years, Kyrgyzstan has not attracted a large community of international humanitarian aid agencies, although international NGOs channeling aid for democratic initiatives have provided support to local NGOs. The acute local awareness of ethnic tensions on its own territory and in the region has prompted the emergence of several NGOs which focus on issues relevant to forced migration. One of these is the Kyrgyz-American Bureau on Human Rights and the Rule of Law, which has representatives in Osh, Jalal-Abad and Naryn, who seek to reduce tensions before conflicts can arise. Ethnic tensions in the southern region are also monitored by the Kyrgyz Peace Research Center, which is working on methods of conflict prevention and reconciliation.

In Bishkek, a center for local NGO support has been established, called InterBilim, which provides all the usual information and assistance to Kyrgyz groups and keeps track of NGO developments in the Central Asian region as well.

In addition to the common obstacle of funding scarcity, local NGOs cite the steep tax rates as an impediment to their operation.

Moldova

Capital: Chisinau

Total area: 33,700 sq. km.

Population: 4,489,657 (July 1995 est.)

Ethnic groups: Moldavian/Romanian 64.5%, Ukrainian 13.8%, Russian 13%, Gagauz 3.5%, Jewish 1.5%, Bulgarian 2%, other 1.7% (1989 figures). Internal disputes with ethnic Russians and Ukrainians in the Dniester region and Gagauz Turks in the south.

Religions: Eastern Orthodox 98.5%, Jewish 1.5%, Baptist, about 1,000 members (1991)

Population growth rate: 0.36% (1995 est.)

Net migration rate: -2.25 migrants/1,000 population (1995 est.)

Displaced persons: est. 350 to several thousand, mostly resettled

Languages: Moldovan (official; virtually the same as the Romanian language), Russian, Gagauz (a Turkish dialect)

GDP per capita: $2,670 (1994 estimate as extrapolated from World Bank estimate for 1992)

Telephone system: 134 telephones/1000 persons (1993)

Brief Context

Moldova's forced migration crisis peaked in 1992, following the outbreak of bloody clashes between Russian-speaking separatists in the sliver of land known as "Dniester area," and the Moldovan government. The bulk of the 70,000-100,000 people who fled that fighting have either returned home or resettled in the region, but the political dispute over control of the self-proclaimed Transdniester Republic remains unresolved.

A fertile land lying between Romania and Ukraine, Moldova is distinguished as the only former Soviet republic to have seen a full-scale battle between the titular nationality and its share of the

25 million ethnic Russians living in the "near abroad." Though the combat lasted only half a year, from March to August 1992, it was fiercely fought with arms and troops from the huge garrison of the Russian 14th Army stationed in the Dniester region, and left as many as several hundred dead.

While Russian nationalists openly supported the secessionist movement, the rest of the former Soviet republics looked on in alarm as Moldova enacted their worst nightmare—the potential for conflict with their own Russian-speaking minorities.

As in other republics which have suffered upheaval and dislocation, the crisis in Moldova traces its roots to historical injustices felt by three main ethnic groups within its borders, which aired during the political opening of the late 1980s.

Moldovans, as others in the USSR, were seeking a national revival of their Romanian-based language and traditions which were thwarted after the Soviet annexation of the territory (formerly Bessarabia) following World War II. In 1989, they passed Latin-scripted Moldovan as the state language, requiring citizens to meet a fluency test by 1994. This alarmed the Russian speakers, as well as the small Turkish Christian community called the Gagauz, in southern Moldova.

In June 1990, the Supreme Soviet declared Moldova a sovereign state, and in rapid succession, the Gagauz declared themselves an independent republic from Moldova, followed by the Dniester region in September 1990. The first outbreak of violence occurred in November of that year, and escalated into a continuous military conflict by the following March. By late July, multilateral peace-keeping forces were introduced into the region. Though the fighting died down, the OSCE-sponsored peace talks between the two sides have not yet resolved the dispute. And in their separate pursuit, the Gagauz are still demanding greater autonomy.

Political analysts do not view Moldova's war as a purely ethnic conflict, but as one aggravated by the political motives of the two sides, and Russian interference in the dispute.

Non-Governmental Efforts

Relatively few remain displaced out of the tens of thousands who initially fled the fighting, and NGOs working in Moldova are not preoccupied with this problem. Roughly 700 local NGOs are reportedly registered on the republican level, but their status is described to be "in flux" at this time, while a new law on public associations is being considered by the Moldovan parliament.

Although relations with the authorities in Chisinau have been more cooperative than in some republics, one point in the new draft law with which the NGOs take issue is the prohibition of political activity by non-governmental groups. The tax laws, similar to other republics, impose a financial burden on organizations, as does the banking commission of 2-3 percent charged for transfers of foreign currency.

Within several months, a new NGO support center known as "Contact" is due to open, with financial backing from the European Community, the American-based International Foundation for Electoral Systems, and the Open Society Institute.

RUSSIA

Capital: Moscow
Total area: 17,075,200 sq. km.
Population: 149,909,089 (July 1995 est.)
Ethnic groups: Russian 81.5%, Tatar 3.8%, Ukrainian 3%,
Chuvash 1.2%, Bashkir 0.9%, Belarusian 0.8%, Moldavian 0.7%,
other 8.1%
Religions: Russian Orthodox, Muslim, other
Population growth rate: 0.2% (1995 est.)
Net migration rate: 0.7 migrants/1,000 population (1995 est.)
Refugees and asylum seekers: 451,000 (145,000 from Tajikistan,
101,000 from Georgia, 84,000 from Azerbaijan, 121,000 other).
An additional estimated 300,000 forced
migrants entered the Russian Federation.
Internally displaced persons: 450,000 based on Russian government
calculations; international organizations and NGOs estimate the
number of refugees and displaced persons to be three times as large.)
Languages: Russian, other
GDP per capita: $4,820 (1994 estimate as extrapolated from
World Bank estimate for 1992)
Telephone system: 164 telephones/1000 persons

Brief Context

As heir to the mantle of Soviet power, Russia has watched in bewilderment and alarm as hundreds of thousands of ethnic Russians arrived from the turbulent southern republics. Surely, no one was prepared for the early tide of Armenian refugees from the shocking pogroms in Azerbaijan in 1988, but in Moscow the Soviet authorities sympathetically responded by offering them homes in local hotels.

The waves swelled, first from Azerbaijan, then from

Uzbekistan and Tajikistan, scenes of ethnic riots. With each new outbreak of violence, nationalist rhetoric and threats sent thousands of Russians fleeing. Many of them had lived so long in the republics now called the "near abroad," that they had nowhere to call "home" in their own land.

While the Russians (and Russian-speakers such as Tatars) searched for work and housing, another gradual sweep of internal migration was taking place with the breakup of the Soviet Union. Army recruits and officers were sent back to their respective republics; migrant industrial workers left their collapsing factories.

Already unable to cope with the needs of its native population, Russia faced another influx of several hundred thousand people in 1992-1993, fleeing the wars in Tajikistan and the Caucasus. The response to each emergency created a patchwork of remedies as complicated as Russia's politics and society. Trying to get a precise figure of the number of displaced people or refugees from non-Soviet countries is as complex as the raft of laws which have been adopted to deal with them.

In all, migration specialists estimate that some 2.5 million people are displaced in Russia, most of them ethnic Russians. Roughly 400,000 of the internally displaced were uprooted by the war against Chechnya; while the government assisted many to travel on to regions for resettlement, some 70,000 remain in temporary quarters in neighboring Ingushetia and Dagestan.

The growing need for legal instruments to address the problems of citizenship, status, property and compensation in Russia, gave rise to two distinct laws in 1993: one on the rights of refugees, and another on the rights of forced migrants. That year, Russia also signed the 1951 United Nations Convention relating to the Status of Refugees (and its 1967 Protocol). It was intended that these would provide the government's new Federal Migration Service (FMS), formed in 1992, with the laws to carry out its mandate.

But the implementation of these laws has been rife with confusion and contradiction, and has bedeviled everyone who has tried to assist the dispossessed. Existing legislation lacks mechanisms for implementation, and the FMS is hopelessly short on government funds to carry out its mandate to register all the displaced and provide them with temporary assistance.

Non-Governmental Efforts

Before the Federal Migration Service was established in 1992, matters of forced migration were handled on an *ad hoc* basis, often by groups of concerned citizens. The first of these to form an NGO expressly for refugee issues was the Civic Assistance Committee (CAC) in Moscow. Founded in 1990, when the refugees from Azerbaijan started to be forced out of the hotel rooms they had been given, the Civic Assistance Committee operates out of the popular weekly *Literaturnaya Gazeta*.

The CAC raises donations to provide small bits of clothing and money to refugees and forced migrants, runs a legal clinic with volunteer lawyers, and arranges for refugees to be represented in court when necessary. It has also found heartening interest among law students at Moscow State University, who volunteer with the committee, and have helped to renovate a school for refugee children from Chechnya.

In addition to material and legal assistance, the Civic Assistance Committee works closely with a coalition of active NGOs concerned with related aspects of forced migration, including the Memorial Human Rights Center (inspecting refugee sites for those uprooted from Chechnya), Human Rights Watch/ Helsinki, the Russian-American Human Rights Bureau and a Quaker group. Members of the coalition have also actively worked with a parliamentary group in drafting new laws on migrants and refugees.

It is safe to say that these local NGOs are overloaded with work, and some of the most active members hold down full-time jobs in addition. There are several groups that are active in related areas, notably the Soldiers' Mothers Committee and the Moscow Research Center for Human Rights. A few international NGOs provide primary health care to refugees housed in temporary settlements, and these include *Médecins Sans Frontières* and the Women and Family Education Center (Magee Women's Care), which furnish reproductive health services.

As described in Chapter Three, a number of local NGOs in Russia have already reached an advanced level of organization, and this is reflected in the array of training and information which could be of use to people concerned with the causes of forced migration. One local NGO, frequently cited during the research for this book, is the support center known as "Golubka." With five full-time employees, Golubka spends 80 percent of its time outside Moscow, and specializes in training for organizational development and leadership. It has also developed seminars in conflict prevention and reconciliation, and published an anthology on nonviolence which it translated into Russian.

And it is not alone. Other local groups frequently cited for their expertise in training and publishing information useful to NGOs are Raduga and Charities Aid Foundation. The latter recently hosted a seminar for representatives of local groups which deal with refugees as far afield as Abkhazia and St. Petersburg.

Conflicts in Abkhazia, Ingushetia and Chechnya have spawned small, but dedicated groups seeking ways to bring ordinary citizens together from conflicting sides, in order to address the differences that brought (or could bring) them to blows.

Again, it is crucial to recall that most of the NGOs mentioned thus far are based in Moscow, where it is relatively simple to register, establish a bank account, and even influence policy-makers.

But several hundred miles away, the pool of people dedicated to forced migration issues dries up.

One person who has worked with the local NGO sector in the Urals mountain region describes it as a "completely different world, much like Moscow in 1991, although not nearly as developed in NGOs." She has found very little grassroots activity of any kind in that region, and NGOs that try to work in non-political fields, often find cooperation on one government level, and hostility on another.

The contrast between the Urals area and other regions where this NGO official has witnessed far greater grassroots activity can be daunting, and she would advise a new donor to think twice before attempting to begin their work in a setting of chronic frustration.

It is out in the provinces, however, where most of the Russian returnees are sent by the federal authorities, who now encourage them to settle in Siberia and other remote regions, hoping to prevent them from seeking work in the cities. With the exception of two small legal aid branches of the Civic Assistance Committee, and a sparsely funded program of the International Organization for Migration (IOM), the Russians returning from Central Asia and the Caucasus are largely left to fend for themselves.

Some have found a welcome reception from the native-born population in the areas where they have been designated to settle. But others encountered rejection, resentment and envy among the local residents, in part due to the resettlers' relatively higher level of education and living standard in the former republics.

One encouraging development has been the appearance of new organizations among the Russian migrants themselves, in the form of small enterprises aimed at supplying the local settlement. At least 17 such groups have sprung up, according to regional migration experts, who have visited over 150 communities of resettlers from Kaliningrad to Vladivostok.

These "Migrant NGOs," however, face several key obstacles. First, they are physically isolated from each other, due to the official policy of scattering groups in non-urban settings. Some migration experts believe that if they had the means to contact each other—even an electronic mail hook-up—they could form a larger NGO to which they could turn for help.

A second obstacle is the resistance they encounter from some local communities. There are recommendations for training in skills enabling them to find common cause with the local population, who see them as outsiders and a drain on local budget.

Once settled, many migrant groups are hindered by their lack of practice in identifying their most important needs over the medium and long term and, moreover, lack skills in presenting that assessment to a potential donor.

Over the long term, such migrant groups, as with many NGOs in Russia, require training in how to advance their cause by advocating for new legislation and enforcement of existing laws.

Beyond the chronic shortage of funds for non-governmental organizations working in the field of migration, the overwhelming obstacle facing them is the morass of ineffective laws governing the treatment of people uprooted from their homes.

Thousands who should qualify as forced migrants under the 1993 law, also face difficulties obtaining that status; tens of thousands of returnees from former republics have bypassed the Federal Migration Service and simply tried to integrate themselves into a local setting. There, however, they face the additional obstacle of the Soviet-era requirement of a residence permit, formerly called *propiska*, which prohibits unregistered residents, even native-born citizens, from getting work, medical services and pensions.

With the administrative anarchy that has accompanied the break-up of the Soviet Union, official abuse of the *propiska* system has been widespread, with local authorities charging fees reportedly as high as $6,000 for citizens and $60,000 for non-citizens. [7]

In December 1995, a new law entitled "Some modifications and supplements to the Law on Refugees and Law on Forced Migrants," entered into force, intended to improve the rights of refugees. But as a coordinator of the Civic Assistance Committee's legal services says, "The laws are not known, even by the court. I was there as a citizen advisor and presented the refugee's case, and they were surprised! They asked where I got this law, and asked what law it was. I told them and they wrote it all down!"

TAJIKISTAN

Capital: Dushanbe

Total area: 143,100 sq. km.

Population: 6,155,474 (July 1995 est.)

Ethnic groups: Tajik 64.9%, Uzbek 25%, Russian 3.5% (declining because of emigration), other 6.6%

Religions: Sunni Muslim 80%, Shi'a Muslim 5%

Population growth rate: 2.6% (1995 est.)

Net migration rate: -1.44 migrants/1,000 population (1995 est.)

Refugees and asylum seekers: 2,500

Languages: Tajik (official), Russian widely used in government and business

GDP per capita: $1,415 (1994 estimate as extrapolated from World Bank estimate for 1992)

Telephone system: 55 telephones/1000 persons

Brief Context

Fear and physical danger have been the hallmarks of Tajikistan's brief period of independence, and three-and-a-half years after the end of the civil war, the situation in the mountainous republic on the border of China and Afghanistan is still highly unstable. Long beset by decades of poverty and neglect under Soviet rule, the USSR's poorest republic entered a new era of troubles in 1990, when several people were killed in violent rampages by youth gangs through the streets of Dushanbe. Soviet security forces were brought in, and panic swept through the Russian community who had settled in Tajikistan over the decades. Within months, more than 100,000 ethnic Russians packed up and left.

The following year, in the wake of the failed coup in Moscow, anti-Soviet protests erupted against the pro-Kremlin leader in Dushanbe. From that point onward, Tajikistan stumbled from protest to protest until May 1992, when government forces backed by Moscow, clashed with opposition demonstrators, comprised of Islamic groups and democratic intellectuals.

Soon the country was plunged into a civil war, which lasted roughly six months, and pitted ethnic and regional loyalties against each other. The cost to the civilian population was enormous. Paramilitary bands swept through villages and towns, particularly in the southern region of Khatlon, looting, killing, and putting houses to the torch. From 20,000-30,000 people were killed, and roughly 100,000 fled to Afghanistan and other countries. Some 600,000 were internally displaced, and hundreds of people, including intellectuals associated with the opposition, were forced to leave the country.

Since 1993, the majority of people have returned home on their own, and the UNHCR sponsored a repatriation program for some 26,000, with a mandate to ensure their safe return, reconstruction of homes, and help with projects for generating income. International human rights monitors view the repatriation as at least a limited success, as tensions intermittently flare in locations where the returnees are regarded by others as being part of the political opposition. There are still reports of murder, beatings and harassment, but their frequency has dropped significantly.

Conditions in the Pamir region of Gorno-Badakhshan have frequently been critical as supply routes are cut by snowfalls during more than half the year, and government officials view the area as hostile to its rule. From regions in the south, reports have emerged this spring of acute food shortages, and a locust infestation has reportedly destroyed cotton and wheat crops in this impoverished land.

Thousands of refugees remain in camps in Afghanistan, 7,500 under UNHCR mandate, and from 13,000-26,000 under the control of rebel fighters who continue to clash with Russian troops along the frontier. Numerous cease-fires and peace talks sponsored by the United Nations have failed to bring an end to this fighting, and the political and security situation in Tajikistan remains volatile.

Non-Governmental Efforts

In matters of forced migration, a prominent human rights advocate in Dushanbe describes the political dimension of the problem as "extremely complex," making the work of international and local NGOs particularly challenging.

The advocate describes three categories of displaced people needing assistance of one kind or another. The first comprises the population which was not politically aligned, but was uprooted by the civil war. Gradually they have returned to their regions, and need assistance rebuilding their homes and shattered economy. Some of these returnees have formed hybrid "NGOs" as micro-enterprises—independent of state control, but organized to restore some small factories and produce goods needed by the local and returning residents.

The second category of vulnerable people either supports the opposition groups or sympathizes with them. Among them are some of Tajikistan's leading figures in public life—scientists, scholars, and poets—who have seen many of their colleagues assassinated since the outbreak of the war, and live in fear.

The third category of uprooted Tajiks represents the members of the active opposition who have survived the war and government crackdowns. Many remain in exile, not only aiming to return, but determined to share power.

At the height of the war and its aftermath, a range of international governmental agencies and NGOs responded to Tajikistan's refugee crisis, but many of them have scaled down their operations and withdrawn. Local NGOs run the risk of being targeted as "anti-government" if they emerge to take up the slack, let alone try to do any advocating on behalf of the populations in need. The recent murder of the local BBC correspondent added to the string of at least 27 journalists killed since 1992 and attested to the danger of anarchy, crime and political violence prevailing in parts of Tajikistan.

There are, therefore, virtually no local NGOs operating in the field of forced migration and refugees in Tajikistan. According to international human rights officials and relief workers who have lived there, the dangers are too great. When told about the kinds of organizational training seminars going on in Russia, one international relief official grimly laughed and said, "Grant-making and management training? Hah! Training would be good in Tajikistan, only it should be training on how to stay alive."

Without exception, local and international observers stress that the greatest obstacle is the absence of a peace accord. "Peace is the number-one condition for any development of the NGO sector," according to one international NGO official. But he warned of additional obstacles facing groups eager to work in Tajikistan. "Remember that Tajikistan is not Lebanon, and there will not be that kind of explosive return of talent even when the fighting is over. There will have to be massive training and funding of fledgling NGOs, though best on the basis of small grants. Secondly, they'll need an international police force to come in and retrain the police and prosecutor's office."

Indeed, another obstacle facing groups concerned with forced migration is lack of legislation for internally displaced people or returning Tajiks. A law exists only for foreign refugees on Tajik territory. Government ministries, even at the highest levels, lack knowledge of international norms pertaining to IDPs and refugees, and there is a great need for such information to be presented in seminars for government officials.

Additional needs cited by local and international experts interviewed for this report are technical assistance, communications and computers. And in the wake of the barbarity witnessed during the war, women and children in particular are in need of treatment for trauma.

In early March of 1996, one prominent human rights advocate expressed a tiny hint of optimism over a recent sign from the government that it wanted to cooperate with some of the better known figures in Tajik society, perhaps to improve its image in the international community. There were hopes of forming a "citizens committee" which would work on the rights of refugees. Still, any local community activity must be pursued with extreme caution, and confrontation with the authorities must be avoided.

Support for legal assistance will also be needed for people when they return from exile and find they have lost their property. The lawyers for such services do exist, in the Associations for Independent Jurists and Lawyers, but as elsewhere, the funds are lacking.

TURKMENISTAN

Capital: Ashgabat
Total area: 488,100 sq. km.
Population: 4,075,316 (July 1995 est.)
Ethnic groups: Turkmen 73.3%, Russian 9.8%, Uzbek 9%,
Kazakh 2%, other 5.9%
Religions: Muslim 87%, Eastern Orthodox 11%, unknown 2%
Population growth rate: 1.97% (1995 est.)
Net migration rate: -2.92 migrants/1,000 population (1995 est.)
Refugees and asylum seekers: 20,000 unrecognized refugees
from Tajikistan
Languages: Turkmen 72%, Russian 12%, Uzbek 9%, other 7%
GDP per capita: $3,280 (1994 estimate as extrapolated from World
Bank estimate for 1992)
Telephone system: 7.5 telephones/1000 persons

Brief Context

Arid, sparsely populated, and bestowed with vast natural gas reserves, the republic of Turkmenistan has escaped the ethnic unrest of its neighbors. It has also escaped much of the tumult of economic reform, having managed to hold fast to the old order of Soviet times. But like its Central Asian neighbors, Turkmenistan has seen the exodus of Slavs in recent years, meaning a loss of technically skilled labor. The consequences to the economy and society are not yet clear.

Headed by a former Soviet Politburo member who has been criticized for ruling by cult-of-personality, Turkmenistan's authoritarian politics find reinforcement from a conservative culture. It stands out, according to a Western human rights monitor, as a republic with "no civil society."

Non-Governmental Efforts

For a brief period at the close of the 1980s, Turkmenistan, too, experienced a slight political opening, which generated some relatively independent non-governmental activities through popular movements. But this opening was very limited, and came to an end by early 1992.

Since then, surveillance and harassment have produced a virtual vacuum of groups or individuals who might be candidates for NGO activity. Some earlier activists managed to flee to Moscow or Europe; others are in prison. The state controls all civic activity, and strictly curtails any form of endeavor which might be construed as political—let alone related to human rights. Critics of the regime are silenced, arrested, and prevented from leaving the country. During the summer of 1995 more than a thousand people joined a street protest (enormous considering the setting) demanding new elections. Hundreds were arrested, and as of April 1996 many were still locked up.

As Turkmenistan has been so isolated from the processes unfolding elsewhere in the fSU, international human rights monitors stress that it is extremely difficult for Turkmen people to obtain independent, reliable information. They see a very great need for "civil society" initiatives, but a very great challenge posed by the cultural conservatism and government interference.

UKRAINE

Total area: 603,700 sq. km.
Population: 51,867,828 (July 1995 est.)
Ethnic groups: Ukrainian 73%, Russian 22%, Jewish 1%, other 4%
Religions: Ukrainian Orthodox-Moscow Patriarchate, Ukrainian
Orthodox-Kiev Patriarchate, Ukrainian Autocephalous Orthodox,
Ukrainian Catholic (Uniate), Protestant, Jewish
Population growth rate: 0.04% (1995 est.)
Net migration rate: 0.71 migrants/1,000 population (1995 est.)
Refugees and asylum seekers: ca. 5000
Languages: Ukrainian, Russian, Romanian, Polish, Hungarian
GDP per capita: $3,650 (1994 estimate as extrapolated from World
Bank estimate for 1992)
Telephone system: 151.4 telephones/1000 persons

Brief Context

Ukraine is another republic which has suffered steady impoverishment since independence, compounded by its stormy relations with Moscow and the large ethnic Russian population in its eastern region and Crimean peninsula. The situation in Crimea has become the focal point for forced-migration monitors, since the recent return of some 280,000 native Tatars from their forced displacement half a century ago.

Like other "punished peoples," the Crimean Tatars were deported in freight trains in 1944 for alleged collaboration with the Nazis, and were only permitted in 1988 to return. Those who did often found their former homes razed or occupied by the local Slavic population. They have settled on the peninsula, nonetheless, many in miserable shanties. The remaining 250,000 Tatars in Central Asia are expected to return by the close of the decade.

The ethnic makeup of Crimea only compounds the Tatars'

problems, as Russians comprising 70 percent of the population and have actively sought to break from Ukraine and unite with Moscow. The former Soviet Black Sea Fleet, docked at the Crimean port of Sebastopol, has been another point of contention between Kiev and Moscow.

Ukraine also faces the return of its titular nationals from other Soviet republics, but thus far their immigration has been sporadic. Population displacement in Ukraine is not only of political origin, but also stems from the environmental disaster caused in 1986 by the Chernobyl nuclear power plant accident. Still others should be resettled from contaminated areas but must remain there for lack of funds.

Non-Governmental Efforts

Ukraine has a relatively healthy community for NGOs in general, with several hundred registered. Local NGO leaders say one of the greatest obstacles to their work is the expense of finding office space, paying utilities, and using electronic mail. Those that are most active in human rights and forced migration have long-established ties with international supporters. They view prospects for grants from Ukrainian businessmen as limited, because they believe that the newly affluent business class would prefer to make donations to more popular projects in art and culture.

The Crimean Tatars themselves have an active advocacy group which has been pushing their cause in Ukraine, Moscow and various international fora, but one of the greatest obstacles daunting many of them is lack of citizenship. According to Ukrainian law, they are entitled to citizenship, but the government delays in granting this status.

Another obstacle is the shortage of legal experts in the republic who can advise both the Tatars and the government on the rights of indigenous peoples. Local human rights activists have been submitting proposals to the government in Kiev for the resolution of the Tatar problem.

The urgency for that resolution weighs heavily on local NGO observers, who see the stability in the Crimea as dangerously fragile. They fear the potential for a "social and political explosion" there, which they believe was only barely averted at the height of the Russian-Ukrainian tensions in 1992-1993. Thus they see this as a crucial period in which to undertake conflict prevention measures, such as using media channels to dispel anti-Tatar propaganda as it appears.

In recent years, with support from Western civic initiatives funds, NGO support centers have formed in Kiev and a legal publishing group has opened up in the city of Kharkov. Local NGO officials stress the need for new literature and textbooks, aimed at young people, to encourage tolerance toward different ethnic groups in the republic.

UZBEKISTAN

Capital: Tashkent

Total area: 447,400 sq. km.

Population: 23,089,261 (July 1995 est.)

Ethnic groups: Uzbek 71.4%, Russian 8.3%, Tajik 4.7%,

Kazakh 4.1%, Tatar 2.4%, Karakalpak 2.1%, other 7%

Religions: Muslim 88% (mostly Sunnis), Eastern

Orthodox 9%, other 3%

Population growth rate: 2.08% (1995 est.)

Net migration rate: -2.23 migrants/1,000 population (1995 est.)

Refugees and asylum seekers: 50,000 unrecognized

refugees from Tajikistan

Languages: Uzbek 74.3%, Russian 14.2%, Tajik 4.4%, other 7.1%

GDP per capita: $2,400 (1994 estimate as extrapolated from

World Bank estimate for 1992)

Telephone system: 63 telephones/1000 persons

Brief Context

Uzbekistan, the third most populous republic in the former Soviet Union, has managed to stay out of the maelstrom destroying its eastern neighbor Tajikistan, and has maintained a dialogue with Russia. This balance, achieved at a considerable cost to an independent, non-governmental sector, is credited to the authoritarian rule of its president, the former Communist leader, Islam Karimov.

But like its Central Asian neighbors, Uzbekistan has also seen the mass emigration of its skilled Russian-speaking population. In the final months of Soviet rule, a rise in Uzbek national rhetoric frightened the Russian population and ancient communities of Jews who had lived in the trading centers along the Old Silk Route for centuries. The Jews began to emigrate en masse to Israel and the West, and the Russians back to Russia.

Uzbekistan's additional migration patterns are intricately interwoven with the forced deportations by Stalin during the 1940s, as it was the main destination for two "punished peoples": the Crimean Tatars and the Meskhetian Turks from Georgia. Since 1989, it has seen the forced exodus of Meskhetians from the Fergana Valley (see section under Azerbaijan) and the departure of half of its Crimean Tatar population (see Ukraine).

The expulsion of the Meskhetians by rampaging Uzbeks in the Fergana Valley did not bring an end to the tensions in that region, where the traditional Muslim population has been more religious than in other parts of the country.

Typical of a nation lying squarely on the ancient trade route between Europe and Asia, Uzbekistan is a mosaic of ethnic groups, and nationalities issues are never far below the surface. Since the start of the Tajik civil war, tensions have flared in the region of southeastern Uzbekistan, where a large Tajik population has lived for centuries in and around the ancient cities of Samarkand and Bukhara. Occasionally, radical Tajiks have raised an inflammatory proposal to re-assign that region of Uzbekistan to Tajik rule.

Non-Governmental Efforts

Non-governmental organizations in Uzbekistan enjoyed a brief period of freedom around the close of the *glasnost* period in the late 1980s and early 1990s. This period abruptly ended in 1992 with the banning of the leading groups that were successors to Uzbekistan's popular front movements, and progressive crackdown on individuals voicing criticism of President Karimov. The state censorship office controlled the press, and at least one foreign journalist was expelled during that period after trying to meet with opposition leaders.

It is an indication of the climate for NGOs that key human

rights activists and leaders of independent movements have been subjected to the whole range of abuses typical of Soviet era repression—harassment, surveillance, physical assault and imprisonment. Many have been driven into exile in Russia, Turkey and the United States.

There is a near vacuum of independent activity within the borders of Uzbekistan, with the exception of a couple of groups who function openly, but with the awareness of the complexity of the situation. Very recently, the authorities have sought to open channels of discussion with human rights groups. The only group left which currently performs human rights monitoring is the Human Rights Society of Uzbekistan. It publishes a regular bulletin with detailed listings of human rights violations, political prisoners, administrative arrests and arbitrary detentions. The bulletin also lists contacts for local people who might need assistance.

Other leaders of independent movements who are operating in exile are the Moscow-based Society for Assistance in Monitoring Human Rights in Central Asia, and the Washington-based Central Asian Human Rights Information Network, headed by a leader of the banned Birlik movement Abdumannob Polat (formerly Pulatov). Polat left Uzbekistan several months after his own arrest by Uzbek security police in December 1992, when he and several other prominent Uzbeks were abducted from an international human rights conference in Bishkek, and returned to Uzbekistan. Earlier that year Polat's brother, Abdurakhim, also a leader of Birlik, was set upon by a gang wielding iron clubs, and hospitalized for his injuries. He, too, has gone into exile.

There are some efforts to create a fund to assist political prisoners and their families in Uzbekistan, but the opportunities to work as openly as in some other former republics has been limited.

BALTIC REPUBLICS

Estonia

Capital: Tallinn
Total area: 45,100 sq. km.
Population: 1,625,399 (July 1995 est.)
Ethnic groups: Estonian 61.5%, Russian 30.3%, Ukrainian 3.17%,
Belarusian 1.8%, Finn 1.1%, other 2.13% (1989)
Religions: Lutheran, Russian Orthodox
Population growth rate: 0.53% (1995 est.)
Net migration rate: 3.31 migrants/1,000 population (1995 est.)
Refugees and asylum seekers: 100
Languages: Estonian (official), Latvian, Lithuanian, Russian, other
GDP per capita: $6,460 (1994 estimated from 1992 World Bank est.)
Telephone system: 246 telephones/1,000 persons

Latvia

Capital: Riga
Total area: 64,100 sq. km
Population: 2,762,899 (July 1995 est.)
Ethnic groups: Latvian 51.8%, Russian 33.8%, Belarusian 4.5%,
Ukrainian 3.4%, Polish 2.3%, other 4.2%
Religions: Lutheran, Roman Catholic, Russian Orthodox
Population growth rate: 0.5% (1995 est.)
Net migration rate: 3.76 migrants/1,000 population (1995 est.)
Refugees and asylum seekers: 150
Languages: Lettish (official), Lithuanian, Russian, other
GDP per capita: $4,480 (1994 estimated from 1992 World Bank est.)
Telephone system: 240 telephones/1000 persons (1993)

Lithuania

Capital: Vilnius

Total area: 65,200 sq. km.

Population: 3,876,396 (July 1995 est.)

Ethnic groups: Lithuanian 80.1%, Russian 8.6%, Polish 7.7%,
Belarussian 1.5%, other 2.1%

Religions: Roman Catholic, Lutheran, other

Population growth rate: 0.71%(1995 est.)

Net migration rate: not available

Refugees and asylum seekers: not available

Languages: Lithuanian (official), Polish, Russian

GDP per capita: $3,500 (1994 estimate as extrapolated from World
Bank estimate for 1992)

Telephone system: 240 telephones/1,000 persons

Brief Context

From their national movements to free themselves from the
Soviet Union, which annexed them in 1940, Estonia, Latvia and
Lithuania have been traveling on a track of their own, turning
their back on Moscow, and following new opportunities in
Western Europe which other republics have not had.

Despite the relative stability the Baltics have enjoyed, they
have weathered a stormy period over two critical problems in
migration. The first is the question of political status for the resident Russians who outnumbered Latvians and Estonians in many
of their own cities at the time of independence in 1991, and the
fate of refugees and asylum seekers from the "far abroad"
marooned in the former Soviet Union.

On the latter problem, each of the Baltic states has faced as
many as several thousand asylum-seekers from countries such as
Iraq, who enter their territory through Russia, hoping to travel

onward to Europe. Reluctant to encourage them, the Baltics have refrained from signing the UN refugee treaties, and have not formulated national laws outlining procedures for evaluating their claims. To further deter potential asylum seekers, they have detained them on the grounds of illegal entry from Russia. Russia refuses to accept them back.

Many of the third-country nationals are seeking passage to one of the Nordic countries, which hesitate to send arrivals back to the Baltics, knowing that they are likely to be locked up. As several cases have demonstrated during the last three years, the asylum seekers can also be shuttled from Estonia to Latvia, and finally put into jail.

International concern over Estonia's policies mounted in 1994, during a hunger strike by more than 80 Iraqi Kurds. Eventually the Kurds were accepted by Finland, after a request by the Estonian government.

On another issue, Estonia and Latvia faced furious threats of reprisals from their huge Russian populations, emboldened by Moscow, over their restrictive citizenship laws adopted in the furor of independence. Given the high proportion of ethnic Russians in each of their republics, and the sour public sentiment toward the large Soviet military contingents which had been stationed on their territory, the titular nationals passed laws designed to encourage Russians to leave.

Estonia offered automatic citizenship to anyone who had held Estonian citizenship prior to 1940, including their descendants. All others would be "foreigners," who had to pass a language test and wait a period before their application for citizenship would be approved. Non-citizens were barred from voting in the crucial 1992 elections.

Latvia, too, required language proficiency, and placed restrictions on non-citizens from holding certain jobs and taking part in the privatization of property. Under pressure from Russia and the international community, there has been some loosening of these laws, and this year Estonia is expected to issue travel documents to its Russian population.

According to regional migration experts, some 200,000 Russians got citizenship in Latvia, and 150,000 in Estonia. But there is great danger of tensions flaring in industrial centers such as Narva, Estonia, right on the Russian border, and whose population is nearly 98 percent Russian.

In the course of the Russian troop pull-out, and debates over citizenship, there has been some out-migration of Russians from the Baltics. But regional migration experts estimate that 600,000 Russians still live in Latvia and 330,000 in Estonia, and add that there are groups who are "sitting on suitcases waiting to leave." Nationalists in Russia suggest that before long, an independence movement among the ethnic Russians in the Baltics could develop.

Non-Governmental Efforts
To a greater degree than in some of the former Soviet republics, the Baltics are home to very few local NGOs dedicated to migration and refugee issues. In other fields, some NGOs are well organized and only require funding to keep their operations running, whereas others need training and assistance to raise public awareness of their particular mission. One NGO official reported plans being discussed for an NGO Information and Documentation Center supported by European funding.

Surely, the development of public awareness is essential to the goal of averting crises which can lead to forced migration, an issue which indeed stirs the passions of residents on both sides of the ethnic divide. In this regard, the Latvian Center for Human Rights and Ethnic Studies has promoted work in conflict-prevention, and encouraged dialogue between ethnic groups.

There is great work to be done by NGOs in the Baltics to encourage their governments to adopt measures in accordance with international refugee law. In the meantime, NGOs can play a crucial humanitarian role in visiting jailed asylum seekers and improving their conditions.

The leading obstacles confronting local NGOs working in the Baltics reflect the impediments reported around the former Soviet Union—tax policies which hinder NGO growth, time spent on bureaucratic red tape; a lack of management and organizational skill, and a difficult economic situation that preoccupies people who might otherwise be active in the non-profit sector.

Notes

1. Many of the observations in this section owe their source to a communication from Elizabeth McKeon, February 27, 1996.
2. One Russian-based group gets around this by meeting with the unsuccessful applicants and discussing the weaknesses of their proposals with them, so they can try again. It is indeed labor-intensive, but the effort seems to pay off in the general level of trust they enjoy with the applicants.
3. Charities Aid Foundation, *Charity Movement: Russia's Regions,* 1995 p.12.
4 For a detailed description of the survey conducted in Togliatti, Chelyabinsk, Magnitogorsk, Voronezh, Krasnodar, and Irkutsk, see Appendix III for *Charity Movement: Russia's Regions.*
5. Id.
6. *Money and Charity,* July 1995, p 22.
7. Communication from Michael Clayton, March 11, 1996.
8. *Forced Migration Monitor,* September 1995.

APPENDICES

Appendix I: NGOs based in the former Soviet Union

Following is contact information concerning selected NGOs working on issues pertinent to migration, including refugees and IDPs. Although no such list can hope to be authoritative, this compilation should serve as a useful starting point for those interested in migration-related work in the region. Various sources of information were utilized to identify these groups. Inclusion in the list, of course, does not constitute endorsement in any respect by either the Forced Migration Projects or the Open Society Institute.

ARMENIA

Armenian Assembly of America (AAA)
2 Republic Square, Room 105, Yerevan
Phone: (374-2) 515-1060, 529-513, 560-674 Fax: (374-2) 151-059

Armenian Constitutional Rights Protective Center
#1 Lane 3, Narekatsi Street, Yerevan
Phone: (374-2) 287-229
Profile: Supports the defense and promotion of human rights and democracy.

Armenian Sociological Association
#44 Aram Street, Yerevan 375010
Phone: (374-2) 531-096, 530-571 or 573-309
E-mail: root@gevork.arminco.com
Profile: Works on refugee issues, women's rights, democracy, and civil society.

Avangard Humanitarian Research Center
3/2 Sogomon Tarontsi Street, Apt. 16, Yerevan
Phone: (374-2) 553-234, 534-011 or 588-495

Friedrich Ebert Stiftung Foundation
38 Toumanian Street, Apt. 47, Yerevan
Phone: (374-2) 532-895

Fund for Armenian Relief, Inc. (FAR)
Council of Ministers Building, Yerevan
Phone: (374-2) 526-660 Fax: (374-2) 151-074
Profile: Successor to the Diocesan Fund for Armenia's Recovery (DFAR) established after the earthquake in December 1988. FAR serves as the relief agency of the Eastern Diocese of the Armenian Church of America. Engages in humanitarian relief, agricultural development programs, medical programs, and nutrition programs. Mainly involved in food distribution throughout Armenia.

Ghevond Alishan Cultural and Educational Association
(Women's subcommittee for refugee women and children)
25/27 Nalbandian Street, Apt. 7, Yerevan 375010
Phone: (374-2) 585-677 or 561-596
Profile: Works on refugee and women's education issues.

Lawyers Youth Union
24 Khorenatsi Street, Yerevan 375010
Phone: (374-2) 567-779
Profile: Works on human rights issues, and worked with a number of NGOs on the new legislation on NGOs before the Armenian parliament.

NGO Training and Resource Center in Armenia
Mosgovyan 24, #2, Yerevan
Phone: (374-2) 582-606

Norwegian Refugee Council
Phone: (374-2) 587-214 or (374-2) 151-706

Refugee Foundation Charitable Association
37 Anrapetakan Street, Yerevan
Phone: (374-2) 560-687 or 537-941
Profile: Provides legal and humanitarian assistance, and supports human rights publications.

Sakharov Fund
1 Jrashat Street, 4th floor, Yerevan

Phone: (374-2) 561-505, 587-864 or 561-560
Profile: Works on human rights issues, democracy, creating new
legislation, publishing and distributing legal information.

Veradardz Haik
Phone: (374-2) 564-494
Profile: Promotes legal and humanitarian assistance to refugees.

ADRA
1 Amirov Street, Apt. #53, Baku
Phone: (994-12) 937-388 Fax : (994-12) 986-896
E-mail: root@adra.baku.az, root@adra1.baku.az, kuhn@nakhichevan.az
(Naxcivan) or ridley@adra.ganja.az (Gence)
Gence address: 17/ 2nd Pereulok Ganja Street, Gence, Azerbaijan
Phone: (994-12) 60-010
Profile: Distributes food to refugees and IDPs in Gence region and Naxcivan AR.

A Humanitarian Children's Foundation
26 Gala Side Street, Apt. #4, Baku
Phone: (994-12) 926-480 Fax: (994-12) 930-866
Profile: Provides psychological treatment to refugees and IDPs.

Association "The Defense of Rights of Azerbaijan Women"
Injasanat Street, Baku 370004
Phone: (994-12) 921-483, 927-456 or 322-793
Profile: Provides humanitarian and legal aid to refugee women.

"AZBLAGO" Azerbaijan Charitable Society
47-91 Ataturk Avenue, Baku 370069
Phone: (994-12) 622-984
E-mail: azblago@ngonet.baku.az
Profile: Distributes food and non-food materials as aid to refugee children.

Azerbaijan Center "Woman and Development"
30 Telnov Street, Baku
Phone: (994-12) 672-139 Fax: (994-12) 925-699
Profile: Helps refugee women.

Azerbaijan Medical Students' Association (AzerMSA)
19-42 Proyezd 1733, Xocali Street, Yeni Ahmedli, Baku
Phone: (994-12) 640-074 or 945-078 Fax: (994-12) 953-870
E-mail: vuqar@azermsa.baku.az
Profile: Episodic humanitarian aid to refugee youth.

Azerbaijani National Committee of Helsinki Citizens' Assembly
3-11 28th May Street, Baku 370014
Phone: (994-12) 933-378 or 938-148 Fax: (994-12) 987-555
E-mail: hca@ngonet.baku.az
Profile: Aid to refugee children, small enterprise development for
refugees.

Azerbaijan Refugee Society
48-54 Karl Marx Avenue, Baku
Phone: (994-12) 620-646 or 621-798

Benevolence International
9 Buniyat Sardarov Street, Apt. #16, Baku
Phone: (994-12) 926-879 Fax: (994-12) 936-151
E-mail: sikandar@bif.baku.az
Profile: Non-food distribution and income generation projects for
refugees.

"Buta" Children's Humanitarian Foundation
26/4 Qala dongesi, Baku
Phone: (994-12) 926-480
Profile: Psychological rehabilitation for children, through sports and
creative arts. Also interested in conflict resolution and prevention.

CARE International
6 Marcanov Gardashlari Street, Apt. #18/20 and 21/2nd Floor, Baku
Phone: (994-12) 985-754 or 982-031 Fax: (994-12) 980-371
E-mail: root@care.baku.az

I. Aliyev Street
Imisli, Azerbaijan
Phone: (994-154) 559-75
Profile: Humanitarian aid.

Caritas Denmark
1 F. Anirov Street, 12th Floor, Apt. #72, Baku
Phone: (994-12) 984-002 or (871) 682-320-123 (satellite)
Fax: (994-12) 984-002
E-mail: root@care.baku.az
In Imisli: 16. I. Aliyev Street, Imisli
Phone: (994-154) 559-75
Profile: Food distribution to refugees and IDPs.

Diakonie
83 Nizami Street, Block #2, Apt. #1 (3rd Floor), Baku
Phone: (994-12) 940-848 or (873) 682-622-819 (satellite, code is correct)
Fax: (873) 682-622-820 (satellite)
E-mail: larsen@diakoni.baku.az
Profile: Food distribution to preschoolers.

Deutsche Gesellschaft für Technische Zusammenarbeit (GTZ)
26/32 Khagani Street, Apt. #72, block 4, Baku
Phone: (994-12) 988-828   Fax: (994-12) 981-607
Profile: Income generation and shelter provision.

Equilibre
177 Tolstoy Street, Apt. #6, Baku
Phone: (994-12) 941-506   Fax: (994-12) 932-022
Profile: Provision of food and medicines to IDPs throughout Azerbaijan.

Feed the Children
201 S. Rahimov Street, Apt. #37, 3rd Floor, Baku
Phone: (994-12) 931-941   Fax: (994-12) 931-941
Profile: Provision of food to IDP children; some involvement in income-generating activities.

Finland-Azerbaijan Friendship Society
21 Hajibayov Street, Apt. #102, Baku
Phone: (994-12) 932-566   Fax: (994-12) 924-963
Profile: Distribution of Finnish humanitarian aid.

German-Azerbaijan Society
Address: 7-9 Qutquasenli Street, Baku
Phone: (994-12) 932-566 or 394-429   Fax: (994-12) 399-280

Profile: Provides medical treatment to refugees and the poor and also distributes food and clothing.

Global CARE
c/o International Learning Center, 16 Firdovsi Street, Baku
Phone: (994-12) 602-05 (Gence)
E-mail: hfa@globcare.ganja.az
Profile: Distributes medicine to refugees/IDPs from Samux region and helps them begin income-generating schemes.

GOF
Vorovski 7, Chapaev Street, Apt. 4, Baku
Phone: (994-12) 681-984
E-mail: bassam@grf.baku.az
Profile: Distributes food to vulnerable groups and assists with income-generating regimes.

Greater Grace Church of Baku
107 Nizami Street, Apt. #97, P.O. Box 137, 370000 Baku
Phone: (994-12) 932-632 or 392-226 Fax: (994-12) 921-255
E-mail: ggrace@mvan.baku.az
Profile: Organizes daily visits to the disabled elderly, IDPs, and refugees; provides household repairs and medical care.

Hayat
72 Kasim-zade Street, Apt. #90, Baku
Phone: (994-12) 981-119 Fax: (994-12) 981-119
Profile: Distribution of sheep and food.

Human Rights Center of Azerbaijan
150-9 B.Safaroglu Street, 370000 Baku
Phone: (994-12) 947-550 Fax: (994-12) 987-555
E-mail: eldar@hrcenter.baku.az
Profile: Founded in 1993. Monitors human rights situation, including forced migration issues.

International Islamic Relief Organization
1 M. Musfiq Street, Block #500, Baku
Phone: (994-12) 388-497 or 384-51 Fax: (994-12) 989-642
Profile: Humanitarian aid.

INSAN Social and Charitable Center
6-39 Khrebtovaja, Apt. #39, Baku
Phone: (994-12) 661-048 or 388-113 Fax: (994-12) 923-297 or 988-340
E-mail: ngo@isar.baku.az
Profile: Provides food to preschoolers.

International Rescue Committee (IRC)
107 Vidadi Street, Apt. #11, Baku
Phone: (994-12) 981-214, 944-685 or 953-594
Fax: (994-12) 989-355
E-mail: office@irchq.baku.az
Profile: Provides food, shelter, non-food materials, sanitation, and supports income generation projects.

Médecins sans Frontières-Belgium (MSF-Belgium)
14 Mamedaliyev Street, Apt. #20/19, Baku
Phone: (994-12) 981-966 or 933-100 Fax: (994-12) 938-713
Profile: Provides medical and non-food supplies to IDPs and hospitals and runs a structural rehabilitation project for central and regional hospitals.

Médecins sans Frontières-Holland (MSF-Holland)
Address: 4 Sheikh Shamil Street, Apt. #8, Baku
Phone: (994-12) 926-621, 928-249 or 926-618
Fax: (994-12) 926-695
E-mail: azg@msfh.baku.az
Profile: Provides drugs and medical supplies to over 250 hospitals and trains medical personnel.

Médecins du Monde (MDM)
Nizami 98/2, Apt. #16, Baku
Phone: (994-12) 957-743 Fax: (873) 113-1454 (satellite)
Profile: Distributes medical supplies and trains medical personnel.

OXFAM
91 Nizami Street, Apt. #49, Baku
Phone: (994-12) 934-816 Fax: (994-12) 981-301
E-mail: office@oxfam.baku.az
Profile: Provides water, sanitation, and health education.

Relief International
2 Amirov Street, Apt. #44, Baku
Phone: (994-12) 984-276 or 980-567 Fax: (994-12) 980-567
E-mail: root@relief.baku.az
Profile: Humanitarian aid.

Russian Community of Azerbaijan
Phone: (994-12) 926-515
Profile: Humanitarian aid to Russian refugees from Armenia and legal
assistance to migrants to Russia.

Save the Children-Azerbaijan
225 D. Alieva, Apt. #36, Baku
Phone: (994-12) 986-516
E-mail: kabin@save.baku.az

"Vatan" Affiliation of International Society of Meskhetian Turks
135 Inqilab Street, Baku
Phone: (994-12) 649-913
Profile: Humanitarian aid to Meskhetian Turks.

BELARUS

Belarusian Children's Fund (BCF)
Prospekt F. Staryni 31, Minsk 220029
Phone: (0172) 326-267 Fax: (0172) 326-267
E-mail: fund@ccfmsq.minsk.by
Profile: Cooperates with the Christian Children's Fund to deliver
health care to children.

Belarusian League for Human Rights
4 F Skaryna Ave.
220010 Minsk
Phone/Fax: (0172) 686-894

International Humanitarian Foundation (IHF)
Masherov Ave. 1-2-5, Minsk
E-mail: mdhirsh@by.glas.apc.org

For the Children of Chernobyl
14 Starovilenskaya Street, Minsk 220029
Phone: (0172) 341-215 or 342-153 Fax: (0172) 323-258
E-mail: mdhirsh@by.glas.apc.org

The Committee for Children of Chernobyl
Varvasheni Street, Minsk 220005
Phone: (0172) 335-012 or 300-008 Fax: (0172) 395-869
Profile: Assists children who were displaced, or whose health was
affected by the 1986 Chernobyl disaster.

United Way Belarus
E-mail: beluwi@minsk.sovam.com
Profile: NGO support center provides NGO-development training, network-
ing among local NGOs, and legislative lobbying.

ESTONIA

Estonian Foundation Centre
Lai 34/Vaimu 3, Tallinn EE0001
Phone: (372-2) 448-884 Fax: (372-2) 448-884
E-mail: aries.efk@geoz.poptel.org.uk
Profile: The Estonian Foundation Centre was founded by representatives
of 26 Estonian Foundations to lead and coordinate the processes of
reestablishing the non-profit sector in Estonia; to provide information,
resources, and technical support to Estonian philanthropic, educational,
cultural, and environmental organizations; and to assist in the integration
of Estonian organizations into the nonprofit network.

Estonian Institute for Human Rights
Tonismagi 2, Tallinn EE0001
Phone: (372-2) 459-477 Fax: (372-2) 453-334

GEORGIA

A Call to Serve-Georgia (ACTS-Georgia)
6 Chorokhi Street, Tbilisi
Phone: (995-32) 969-133 Fax: (995-32) 953-894

E-mail: actsg@actsg.ge or akag@aod.ge
Profile: A Call to Serve-Georgia delivers and distributes humanitarian aid to refugees, disabled children, and single mothers. ACTS is supported by its US-based affiliate, ACTS International. Its goal is to forge a transition from a partnership humanitarian aid program to a fully self-sufficient NGO able to serve the needs of the displaced and others at risk in Georgia.

All Georgian Association of Human Rights (AGAHR)
32 Dadiania Street, Tbilisi
Phone: (995-32) 663-940
Profile: Aims to protect people from persecution based on political views or ethnic affiliation; uses the media to publicize the cause of human rights.

Association of IDP Women from Abkhazia "Tankhmoba"
Green House, Mushtaedi, Tbilisi
Phone: (995-32) 935-645, 954-497, 351-914 or 740-123
Fax: (995-32) 932-147 or 954-497
E-mail: giatm@cippd.ge or marina@bji.ge
Profile: Founded in January 1994, the Association helps protect internally displaced women and provide them with psychological, social, and medical care. The Association conducts surveys to pinpoint areas of need and works with other local and foreign NGOs.

Association of Refugee Teachers from Abkhazia "Chiragdani"
8 Tsereteli Street, Room #55, Tbilisi
Phone: (995-32) 341-803, 350-613 or 393-286
Profile: Founded in June 1994, the Association works to improve the social and living conditions of refugee teachers. The Association has distributed humanitarian aid among refugee teachers and has helped them find work.

Association of Women Refugees from Abkhazia (AWRA)
#7, Building #13, Nutsubidze MD #4, Tbilisi
Phone: (995-32) 313-611

Caritas Georgia
5 Marganishvili Street, Tbilisi
Phone: (995-32) 969-164 or 969-181
Profile: Combats extreme poverty. Distributes food to victims of disasters, orphans, hospitals, and pensioners regardless of nationality or religion. Caritas plans to experiment with small enterprise development for vulnerable groups.

Caucasian Institute for Peace, Democracy and Development (CIPDD)
PO Box 4 (158), 380008 Tbilisi
Phone: (995-32) 954-723 Fax: (995-32) 954-479 or 950-855
E-mail: cipdd@cipdd.ge or cipdd@iphil.kheta.georgia.su

Center for Humanitarian Programmes
36 Gogol Street, Sukhumi, Abkhazia
Phone: (995-32) 205-67 Fax: (8832) 230-76
E-mail: center1@glas.apc.org
Profile: Provides psychological rehabilitation for women and children
displaced and traumatized by war. Holds educational seminars on theme
of conflict resolution.

Center of Social and Humanitarian Initiatives (CSHI)
8 Lermontov Street, Tbilisi
Phone: (995-32) 935-645
Profile: Helps vulnerable groups such as refugees, orphans, and other victims
of armed conflict. The Center has an anti-tuberculosis project and a social
security project designed to help families that lost their main wage earner
during the war.

Eduard Shevardnadze Foundation
16 Rustaveli Avenue, Tbilisi
Phone: (995-32) 931-160 or 984-431
Fax: (995-32) 933-199 or (0495) 1511-3060, ext. 171 (satellite)
Profile: Supports various programs of humanitarian assistance for vulnerable
people, including refugees and IDPs.

Georgian Charity and Health Foundation (GCHF)
30 K. Gamsakhurdia Ave., Tbilisi
Phone: (995-32) 387-407 or 386-170
Profile: Assists the poor, veterans, refugees, invalids, and victims of natural
disasters.

Georgian Republic Committee on Refugees (GRCR)
Address: Tbilisi
Profile: Founded in 1992. The Committee registers refugees and
maintains a database on refugees and internally displaced persons. Studies
have been conducted on problems facing refugees. GRCR collaborates with
international NGOs as well as with governmental organizations.

Georgian Women's Council (GWC)
14 Kostava Street, Tbilisi
Phone: (995-32) 997-990
Profile: Assists internally displaced women and children and addresses domestic issues.

Georgian Young Lawyers Association (GYLA)
5 Dadiana Street, Tbilisi
Phone: (995-32) 987-016
E-mail: lawyer@cec.ge
Profile: Provides free legal consultation for Georgian NGOs and helps establish connections between the business and NGO communities.

Georgian Youth Committee of Helsinki Citizen's Assembly
Apt. 31, Building 112, Gldani Md #4, Tbilisi
Phone: (995-32) 680-434

Helsinki Citizens Assembly of Georgia
Phone: (995-32) 961-514
Profile: Works with refugees and IDPs and plans reconciliation meetings between people from Georgia, South Ossetia, and Abkhazia.

International Center for Conflict and Negotiation (ICCN)
161 Chavchavadze Avenue, Tbilisi
Phone: (995-32) 223-618 or 341-195
E-mail: iccn@aod.ge
Profile: ICCN explores ways to avoid future violent conflict in the region.

International Fund "Multiple Assistance to Georgia" (MAG)
Rm. 706, 7 Ingorokva Street, Tbilisi
Phone: (995-32) 397-437 or 987-847
Profile: Provides humanitarian assistance and medical supplies. Coordinates NGO training. Participates in UN-sponsored conflict resolution exercises.

International Society "Women of Georgia for Peace" (ISWGP)
20, Ateni Street, Tbilisi
Phone: (995-32) 222-066 Fax: (995-32) 985-778
Profile: Founded in May 1992. The Society's 1000 members work to support peaceful conflict resolution in Georgia while providing humanitarian assistance to the victims of war.

International Telecommunications and Information Center (ITIC)
Room 102, Department of City Projects
89/24 Agmashenebeli Ave, Tbilisi
Phone: (995-32) 952-034
E-mail: root@itic.ge
Profile: A clearinghouse for NGOs which provides training in computers, management, and English language. Publishes NGO newsletter called "New Georgia" (formerly "Grassroots").

KAZAKHSTAN

Almaty Helsinki Committee
Mkr. Koktem 1, dom 26, kv. 43, 480070 Almaty
Phone: (3272) 477-079 Fax: (3272) 477-079
Profile: Human rights monitoring and advocacy.

Kazakhstan-American Bureau on Human Rights and Rule of Law
Almaty
Phone 3272 62 68 11
fax 3272 67 66 10
email: omaz@abexc.alma-ata.su

Central Asian Sustainable Development Information Network (CASDIN)
Almaty
E-mail: network@glas.apc.org
Profile: NGO support center, produces newsletter and provides information and training. Offers local NGOs use of computer and telephone.

KYRGYZSTAN

Fund for Legal Initiatives
Bokonbaeva 12, Bishkek 720017
Profile: NGO development.

InterBilim
Phone: (3312) 268-898 Fax: (3312) 226-86
Profile: NGO clearinghouse/support center; provides information and training to local NGOs in region.

Kyrgyz-American Bureau on Human Rights and Rule of Law
175 Sovetskaya Street, Bishkek
Phone: (3312) 265-754 Fax: (3312) 263-865
E-mail: na@rights.bishkek.su
Profile: Created after the international conference on "Human Rights and
the Fate of Nations in Central Asia" held in 1992. The Bureau monitors
human rights violations, lobbies the government for improved human rights
conditions, and works with international human rights organizations.

Kyrgyz Peace Research Center
Phone: (3312) 280-423
E-mail: root@kprc.bishkek.su
Profile: Conflict prevention and reconciliation between ethnic groups in
southern Kyrgyzstan.

LATVIA

Latvian Center for Human Rights and Ethnic Studies
Postal address: Raina Bulv 19, LV-1568 Riga
Office address: Vecpilsetas iela 13/15, 4th floor, Riga
Phone: (3712) 211-097 Fax: (371) 882-0113

MOLDOVA

Movement of Refugees From Transdniestria
4 Anton Pann Street, Hotel Zarea #1209, Chisinau
Phone: (0422) 248-240 or 731-846 Fax: (0422) 228-288

**Charity School for Child Orphans, Refugees, and
Those from Large and Poor Families**
Calea Lesilor 33, Chisinau
Phone: (3732) 233-158
Profile: Provides training in sewing and word processing for people
displaced by the conflict in the Transdniester area.

Andrei Sakharov Foundation
Zemlyanoi val (Chkalova) 48b, Suite 62, 107120 Moscow
Fax: (095) 299-0232
E-mail: yuriy@sakharovfound.msk.su

Association for Assistance to Refugees in Saint Petersburg
Phone: (812) 314-2830

Catholic Relief Services (CRS)
56 Sheronova Street, room 302, 680013 Khabarovsk
Phone: (4212) 212-268 or 338-566
E-mail: spatz@crs.khabarovsk.su

Center for Peacemaking-Moscow
Ulitsa Malaya Filosofskaya, Dom 16, Kor.1, Kv. 74, Moscow
Phone: (095) 144-5408
Profile: Provides support to war refugees in northern Caucasus.

Charities Aid Foundation
Ulitsa Yakovoapostolsky Per. #10, 103064 Moscow
Phone: (095) 928-0557 Fax: (095) 975-2190
E-mail: lenay@glas.apc.org
Profile: NGO clearinghouse which provides training in NGO development
and management; commissions and publishes in-depth studies on social
problems and areas of need for NGO humanitarian work.

Civic Assistance Committee
c/o Literaturnaya Gazeta, Kostiansky Per. 13, 103811 Moscow
Phone: (095) 208-9462
Profile: Assistance to refugees and migrants, including provision of
clothing, money and legal assistance and advice. The Committee also
lobbies lawmakers on refugee and migration issues.

Compassion
Komsomolskiy prospekt, 9 apt 45, Moscow
Phone: (095) 245-2209 Fax: (095) 923-4778 or 245-2209
Profile: Provides health services to former political prisoners and counseling
for victims of violent conflicts.

Coordinating Council for Aid to Refugees and Displaced Persons
c/o Literaturnaya Gazeta, Kostiansky Per. 13, 103811 Moscow
Phone: (095) 208-8805 Fax: (095) 200-0238
Profile: Umbrella organization for certain groups working in Russia with refugees and migrants.

Eurasia Foundation
ul. Volkhonka 14, 4th floor, 119842 Moscow
Phone: (095) 956-1235 Fax: (095) 956-1239
E-mail: clmoscow@glas.apc.org

Friends House Moscow
Bolshoi Nikolopieskovsky Per, Dom 3, Apt 46, 121002 Moscow
Phone: (095) 241-3487
E-mail: fhm@glas.apc.org
Profile: Works with local groups helping refugees and IDPs, monitoring human rights, and promoting nonviolent methods of conflict resolution and reconciliation.

Golubka Center for Experiential Education for Social Change and Democracy
Ulitsa Garibaldi 11-76, Moscow
Phone: (095) 134-0295 Fax: (095) 134-0295
E-mail golubka@glas.apc.org
Profile: NGO support center offering wide range of training in organizational development, strategic planning and fundraising for NGOs.

Human Rights Watch/Helsinki
Perviy Basmanny Tupik dom 4, kv 72
Phone: (095) 267-8327 Fax: (095) 265-4448
E-mail: hrwmosc@glas.apc.org
Profile: Monitors broad range of human rights in former Soviet republics, petitions governments for action on violations of the rights of prisoners, refugees, forced migrants, civilians caught in conflict zones; and publishes detailed reports of fact-finding missions throughout the former Soviet Union

Ingush Women's Association
Ulitsa Kartoyeva 81, Nazran
Phone: (8234) 237-16
Profile: Works with Ingush IDPs from 1992 conflict in North Ossetia; seeks

conflict resolution between members of displaced Ingush community and former North Ossetian neighbors.

Interlegal
ul. Marii Ulianovoy, 16/1, P.O. Box 450, Moscow
Phone: (095) 138-4408 Fax: (095) 138-5686
E-mail: interlegal@glas.apc.org
Profile: Researches and disseminates information to the NGO sectors in Russia, Ukraine, Kazakhstan, and Uzbekistan; reports on government-NGO relations, the legal environment for NGOs, and provides legal assistance.

IREX
Khlebniy pereulok 8, Moscow
Phone: (095) 290-6233 or 290-5878 Fax: (095) 202-4449
E-mail: irexmos@glas.apc.org
Profile: IREX is creating a computer network linking NGOs throughout Russia, and will sponsor discussion groups and monthly seminars on NGO training and management.

Memorial Society
Maly Karetny Pereulok 12, 103051 Moscow
Phone: (095) 299-1180
E-mail: memhrc@glas.apc.org
Profile: Monitoring and advocacy regarding human rights, published a directory of human rights organization in the former Soviet Union.

Migrant Self-Help Groups
Profile: Assist Russians returning from other republics, and includes groups in Saratov region and Ekaterinberg. Contact them through IOM-Moscow office.

Moscow Research Center for Human Rights
Louchnikov Lane 4, Apt. 5, 103982 Moscow
Phone: (095) 206 0923 Fax (095) 206-8853
E-mail: hrcenter@glas.apc.org
Profile: Direct assistance to persons denied permission to emigrate.

Nizhny Novgorod Charitable Fund
Ulitsa Minina, 6, Nizhny Novgorod
Phone: (8312) 603-005, 603-008 or 337-227 Fax: (8312) 340-504
Profile: Initially worked with small business loans, and now supporting

NGOs in the field of microenterprise development. The Fund provides training and is creating a network of NGOs in the Nizhny Novgorod region.

Nonviolence International-NIS
Louchnikov Lane 4, Room 2, 103982 Moscow
Profile: Conflict prevention and reconciliation in Southern Russia.

Pamir Relief and Development Program
Mosfilmskaya ulitsa 11, Apt. 1, Moscow
Phone: (095) 146-9524
Profile: Provides training and small grants to local NGOs involved in community development. Cooperates with the Aga Khan Foundation.

Raduga
3-d Frunzenskaia 1-73 119270 Moscow
Phone: (095) 268-4035
E-mail: raduga@glas.apc.org
Profile: Publishes brochures and newsletters on the work of nongovernmental organizations, charitable and voluntary activity, and educational topics.

Residence
Phone: (095) 923-7862 Fax: (095) 923-7776
Profile: Policy research and advising; works with local groups helping IDPs in Novgorod and Voronezh.

Save the Children Federation
13/2 Ordhonikidze Street, 15th Floor, Moscow
Phone: (095) 958-5130
Profile: Received 3-year USAID grant in September 1994 to manage and coordinate a "Russian Civic Initiatives for Democratic and Economic Reform Program." This program is designed to increase the capacity of the NGO community in Russia and to strengthen its fundraising capacity. SC cooperates with the Center for Democracy and the Counterpart Foundation. The latter will operate a clearinghouse of information on NGO activities in Russia.

Siberian Center for the Support of Social Initiatives
Prospekt Karla Marksa 57, Kom. 702, Novosibirsk
Phone: (3832) 464-532
Profile: NGO Support Center for Siberia with regional offices in

Gorno-Altaisk, Omsk, Krasnoyarsk, Tomsk, Novokuznetsk, Barnaul, and Kemerovo. Organizes seminars and training sessions on all aspects of managing an NGO including funding, accounting, legal aspects, publicity, computer and telecommunication training, relations with the press, networking with other NGOs, and applications for grants.

Sluzhenie
Pamirskaya 11, GCP 1005, 603600 Nizhny Novgorod
Phone: (8312) 522-448 or 522-889 Fax: (8312) 520-305
Profile: Support center for NGOs in the Nizhny Novgorod region.

**Tatarstan Republican Foundation for Assistance
to Refugees and Forced Migrants**
Phone: (8432) 327-390 or 325-067

United Way International-Russia
ul. Gilyarovskaya, 5, Moscow
Phone: (095) 208-8514
Profile: UWI compiles directories about NGOs in Russia. Training programs are run through a new Moscow Volunteer Center. Aims to establish similar centers in other republics.

Urals Association of Refugees
Phone: (3432) 518-779
Profile: Provides small business training for IDPs.

TAJIKISTAN

CARE
Rudaki Street, Apts. 4 & 5
Dushanbe
Phone: (3772) 21-17-83 or 24-17-64 Fax: (3772) 21-17-78

"Citizens Committee"
Phone: (3772) 24-82-33 Fax: (3772) 21-03-62 or (851) 15-15-353

Pamir Relief and Development Program
Address: Gorno-Bakhshansky Region, Khorog
Phone: (377) 91-02-719

Profile: Provides local NGO training and assistance. Cooperates with the Aga Khan Foundation.

Human Rights Watch/Helsinki
Rudaki Street 64, Apt. 26, Dushanbe
Phone: (3772) 21-52-69 Fax: (3772) 21-52-69
E-mail: hrwtajik@glas.apc.org
Profile: See Human Rights Watch/Helsinki in the Russia section.

UKRAINE

Association of Nations of Crimea
Ulitsa Gogolya, Simferopol
Phone: (0652) 279-460 or 279-490
Profile: Assists all returnees, including Bulgarians, Greeks and Tatars.

Center for Pluralism at the Pylyp Orlyk Institute for Democracy
40 A Moskovskaya Street, 252015 Kyiv
Phone: (380 44) 290-7756 or 290-6563 Fax: (380 44) 290-6464
E-mail: orlyk@orlyk.gluk.apc.org
Profile: Human rights monitoring and advocacy

Local Charitable Organization Association
Kharkov
Phone: (0572) 435-229
E-mail: bomar@gjarn.kharkov.ua
Profile: NGO regional service center; provides humanitarian assistance, organizational development seminars and lobbies government.

Migration Problems Research Center
26/28 Kudryavska Street, Rm 103, Kyiv
Phone: (380 44) 212-4895 Fax: (380 44) 212-4895
Profile: Analyzes migration issues in Ukraine and lobbies lawmakers on issues regarding refugees, displaced persons, and migrants.

The Rebirth of Crimea Foundation
Pushkina Street, Bakhchisaray, Crimea
Phone: (06554) 425-79
Profile: Works with Tatar returnees.

Ukrainian Affiliates of GJARN
c/o Reg. Red Cross Committee
Novgorodskaya ul. 4, Kharkov
Phone: (0572) 433-856 Fax: (0572) 433-856 or 452-140
or: ul. Sverdlova 6, Apt. 313, 320101 Dnipropitrivsk
Phone: (0562) 783-443
E-mail: levin@infocom.kharkov.ua or gjardniepr@gluk.apc.org
Profile: GJARN runs humanitarian assistance programs on a non-sectarian basis. Programs include refugee resettlement and support for victims of the Chernobyl disaster.

Ukrainian-American Bureau on Human Rights
E-mail: root@khghr.kharkov.ua

Ukrainian Center for Human Rights
Phone: (380 44) 227-2398 Fax: (380 44) 227-2398
E-mail: pravo@ULF.freenet.kiev.ua

Xylon Publishers
Kharkov
Phone: (0572) 432-738
E-mail: urinfo@xylon.kharkov.ua
Profile: Published handbook for NGOs on how to register with government.

UZBEKISTAN

American Legal Consortium (ALC)
ul. Kodiri 11, Room 202, Tashkent 700011
Fax: (3712) 41-86-06
E-mail: alc@glas.apc.org

Central Asian Free Exchange (CAFE)
Prospekt Navoii 48, Tashkent 700021
Phone: (3712) 45-16-72 or 93-39-23 Fax: (3712) 42-28-82
E-mail: mala@malstead.silk.glas.apc.org
Profile: Provides humanitarian assistance and investigates environmental health problems.

Human Rights Society of Uzbekistan
Chilanzaya D20A, building 1, Apt. 70, Tashkent 700156
Phone: (3712) 16-13-42
Profile: Closely monitors human rights and publishes "Information Bulletin" containing detailed lists of political prisoners, detentions, and restrictions on free association.

Project on Economic Reform and Development in Central Asia
Address: P.O. Box 475, Tashkent 700047
E-mail: mcdonald@silk.glas.apc.org

Society for Assistance in Monitoring Human Rights in Central Asia
Moscow
Phone: (095) 270-2463   Fax: (095) 277-0646
Profile: Human rights monitoring by Central Asians forced into exile.

Appendix II: Western-Based NGOs and Clearinghouses

Following is contact information concerning Western-based NGOs and clearinghouses working on issues pertinent to migration, including refugees and IDPs. Various sources of information were utilized to identify these groups. This compilation should serve as a useful starting point for those interested in migration-related work in the region. Inclusion in the list, of course, does not constitute endorsement in any respect by either the Forced Migration Projects or the Open Society Institute.

A Call to Serve International (ACTS)
895 Kifer Road, PO Box 60788
Sunnyvale, CA 94088-0788
Phone: (408) 245-4905, 245-4907

Adventist Development and Relief Agency International (ADRA)
12501 Columbia Pike
Silver Spring, MD 20904
Phone: (301) 680-6380 Fax: (301) 680-6370
Profile: Assists displaced persons in Azerbaijan; runs a microenterprise project in Kazakhstan, a health center in Kyrgyzstan, and soup kitchens in Russia and Ukraine.

Aga Khan Foundation USA
1901 L Street, NW, Suite 700
Washington, DC 20036
Phone: (202) 293-2537 Fax: (202) 785-1752
E-mail: 71075.1561@compuserve.com
Profile: Began in 1992 with an emergency humanitarian assistance program in Tajikistan. In the long-term, AKF supports activities in health, education, and rural development. AKF has established a Tajik partner NGO.

American Bar Association/Central and East European Law Initiative
1800 M Street, NW, Suite 200 South
Washington, DC 20036
Phone: (202) 331-4070 Fax: (202) 862-8533
Profile: Places lawyers in volunteer positions with organizations throughout the former Soviet Union and Central and Eastern Europe.

American Red Cross (ARC)
431 18th Street, NW
Washington, DC 20006
Phone: (202) 737-8300 Fax: (202) 728-6404
Profile: The American Red Cross works with the Red Cross Red Crescent Societies to distribute medical supplies, food, and technical assistance to local Red Cross/Red Crescent societies in the former Soviet Union.

America's Development Foundation (ADF)
101 North Union Street, Suite 200
Alexandria, VA 22314
Phone: (703) 836-2717 Fax: (703) 836-3379
Profile: ADF provides assistance to NGOs in the area, the Moscow Research Center for Human Rights, and the Ukrainian Center for Human Rights.

Armenian Assembly of America
122 C Street, NW, Suite 350
Washington, DC 20001
Phone: (202) 393-3434
Profile: The AAA has been working in Armenia since February 1988 on a variety of projects, including training for NGOs.

CARE
151 Ellis Street
Atlanta, GA 30335
Phone: (404) 681-2552 Fax: (404) 577-4515
Profile: Care distributes food and medical supplies in the former Soviet Union and provides NGOs with technical assistance. CARE-USA has offices in Moscow, St. Petersburg, Ekaterinburg, and Perm, and in Armenia, Azerbaijan, and Georgia.

Center for Civil Society International
2929 Blakeley Street, Seattle, WA 98105-3120
Phone: (206) 523-4755 Fax: (206) 523-1974
E-mail: ccsi@u.washington.edu

Central Asian Human Rights Information Network (CAHRIN)
(Subdivision of Union of Councils of Soviet Jews)
1819 H Street, NW, Ste 230, Washington, DC. 20006
Phone: (202) 775-9770 Fax (202) 775-9776

E-mail: 4201773@mcimail.com
Profile: Monitors human rights violations in Central Asia.

Charities Aid Foundation (CAF)
114/118 Southhampton Row, London WC1B 5AA, U.K.
Phone: (44 171) 400-2300
Profile: See Charities Aid Foundation under Russia.

Christian Children's Fund
2821 Emerywood Parkway, (PO Box 26227)
Richmond, VA 23261
Phone: (804) 756-2700 Fax: (804) 756-2718

PO Box 2100
Route de Ferney 150, 1211 Geneva 2, Switzerland
Phone: (41 22) 788-9077, 788-9082 Fax: (41 22) 788-9083
Profile: see Belarusian Children's Fund under Belarus.

Church World Service
475 Riverside Drive
New York, NY 10115-0050
Phone: (212) 870-2257

Counterpart Foundation, Inc.
910 17th Street, NW #328
Washington, DC 20006
Phone: (202) 296-9676 Fax: (202) 296-9679
Profile: Counterpart functions as a clearinghouse for USAID and works with a Russian partner, Russian Care. Counterpart is a member of the Russian NGO Sector Support Program (NGOSSP), with Save the Children, the Education Development Center, and the Center for Democracy.

Direct Relief International (DRI)
27 S. La Patera Lane
Santa Barbara, CA 93117-3251
Phone: (805) 964-4767
Profile: DRI delivered medical supplies and equipment in Armenia after the 1988 earthquake. In 1991, it launched a Multi-Level Health Support and Training Program in the country. DRI has also provided relief assistance to refugees and displaced persons in Azerbaijan and Georgia.

InterAction
1717 Massachusetts Avenue, NW, Suite 801
Washington, DC 20036
Phone: (202) 667-8227 Fax: (202) 667-8236
Profile: InterAction is a coalition of over 150 private and voluntary organizations working in international development, refugee assistance and protection, disaster relief and preparedness, and public policy.

International Catholic Migration Commission (ICMC)
1319 F Street, NW, Suite 820
Washington, DC 20004
Phone: (202) 393-2904
Profile: ICMC provides training to former military officers in Novgorod, Pskov, Volgograd, and Nizhny Novgorod.

International Center for Not-for-Profit Law (ICNL)
1511 K Street, NW, Suite 723
Washington, DC 20005
Phone: (202) 624-0766 Fax: (202) 624-0767
E-mail: dcinl@aol.com
Profile: ICNL provides legal analysis of NGO-related laws throughout the former Soviet Union and specializes in the Central Asian legal systems.

International Orthodox Christian Charities (IOCC)
711 West 40th Street, Suite 356
Baltimore, MD 21211
Phone: (410) 243-9820 Fax: (410) 243-9824
E-mail: iocc@igc.apc.org
Profile: IOCC provides training to Russian NGOs and sponsors research on refugees and displaced persons. IOCC initiated a partnership with the Georgian Orthodox Church in November 1993, establishing a Humanitarian Aid Unit (HAU) to distribute relief supplies in Georgia.

International Rescue Committee
122 East 42nd Street
New York, NY 10168-1298
Phone: (212) 551-3060 or 551-3070 Fax: (212) 551-3185
Profile: The IRC's programs include sanitation, housing, infrastructure repair, food distribution, and reforestation. IRC has programs for IDPs in Azerbaijan, Georgia, and Tajikistan.

IREX—International Research and Exchanges Board
1616 H Street, NW, Washington, DC 20006
Phone: (202) 628-8188 Fax: (202) 628-8189
E-mail: irex@info.irex.org

ISAR (formerly Institute for Soviet-American Relations)
1601 Connecticut Avenue, NW, Suite 301
Washington, DC 20009
Phone: (202) 387-3034 Fax: (202) 667-3291
E-mail: isar@igc.apc.org
Profile: ISAR publishes the quarterly journal "Surviving Together" containing articles on environmental and women's issues, civil society, culture, and other topics related to Eurasia. It also supports grassroots NGO development throughout the former Soviet Union and has offices in Georgia, Azerbaijan, Kazakhstan, Russia, and Ukraine.

Magee Womancare International
c/o Magee Women's Hospital
300 Halket Street
Pittsburgh, PA 15213
Phone: (412) 641-1189 Fax: (412) 641-1221
Profile: Works with refugees around Moscow in partnership with a Russian hospital.

Médecins Sans Frontières USA/Doctors Without Borders USA (MSF)
30 Rockefeller Plaza, Suite 5425
New York, NY 10112
Phone: (212) 649-5961 Fax: (212) 246-8577
and: 1999 Avenue of the Stars, Suite 500
Los Angeles, CA 90067
Phone: (310) 551-4072 Fax: (310) 553-3928
Profile: Assists victims of armed conflict or natural disasters. MSF works in Azerbaijan, Georgia, Armenia, and the Northern Caucasus region of Russia.

Médecins Sans Frontières France (MSF)
8 Rue St. Sabin, 75011 Paris, France
Phone: (33 1) 4021-2929 Fax: (33 1) 4806-6868
Profile: Assists victims of armed conflict or natural disasters. MSF works in Azerbaijan, Georgia, Armenia, and the Northern Caucasus region of Russia.

National Association of Social Workers
750 First Street, NE, Suite 700
Washington, DC 20002-4241
Phone: (202) 408-8600 Fax: (202) 336-8310
E-mail: ekelly@capcom.net
Profile: Builds NGO capacity in the social sector and provides NGO training.

Network of East-West Women
1621 Connecticut Avenue, NW, Suite 301
Washington, DC 20009
Phone: (202) 332-4840 Fax: (202) 332-4865
E-mail: newwdc@igc.apc.org
Profile: Communication network organizing projects, training workshops, conferences, and information exchanges on topics related women's issues.

OXFAM
274 Banbury Road,
Oxford OX27 DZ, U.K.
Phone: (44 186) 531-1311 Fax: (44 186) 531-2600 r. 380

Salvation Army World Service Office (SAWSO)
615 Slaters Lane, Box 269
Alexandria, VA 22313
Phone: (703) 684-5528
Profile: SAWSO distributes food aid to vulnerable groups in Georgia, especially displaced persons.

Save the Children Federation
54 Wilton Road, PO Box 950
Westport, CT 06881
Phone: (203) 221-4000 Fax: (203) 221-4210
Profile: Administers a multi-million dollar "civic initiatives" program for USAID, to develop local NGO activities in the former Soviet Union.

United Methodist Committee on Relief (UMCOR)
475 Riverside Drive
New York, NY 10115
Phone: (212) 870-3816
Profile: UMCOR works in Georgia and Armenia to distribute pharmaceuticals.

United Way International
701 North Fairfax Street
Alexandria, VA 22314-2045
Phone: (703) 519-0092 Fax: (703) 519-0097
E-mail: uwi@igc.apc.org
Profile: Serves as clearinghouse for information on the NGO sector in Russia; publishes NGO newsletter; directory; computer database; training workshops. United Way International also runs an NGO support center in Belarus.

Volunteers in Overseas Cooperative Assistance
50 F Street, NW, Suite 1075
Washington, DC 20001
Phone: (202) 383-4961 Fax: (202) 783-7204

World Learning Inc.
1015 Fifteenth Street, NW, Suite 911
Washington, DC 20005
Phone: (202) 408-5420 Fax: (202) 898-1920
E-mail: 5517826@mcimail.com
Profile: Administers a multi-million dollar project (PVO/NIS) for USAID to develop NGO activities in the former Soviet Union.

Appendix III: Suggested Bibliography on NGO Experience

This bibliography is intended as a reference guide for NGOs wishing to establish operations in the former Soviet Union. Some of these materials have been relied upon in preparing this report; others are listed because they might be useful aids in the organizational and institutional development of new NGOs in the region.

BOOKS

Bryson, J. *Strategic Planning for Public and Non-Profit Organisations: A Guide to Strengthening and Sustaining Organizational Achievement.* London: Jossey-Bass, 1988.

Butler, P. and Wilson, D. *Managing Voluntary and Non-Profit Organisations: Strategy and Structure.* London: Routledge, 1990.

Charity Movement: Russia's Region. Moscow: Charities Aid Foundation, 1995 (in Russian).

Drukker, P. *Managing the Non-Profit Organization: Principles and Practices.* New York: HarperCollins, 1990.

Egland, J. and Krebs, T, eds. *Third World Organizational Development: A Comparison of NGO Strategies.* Geneva: Henry Dunant Institute, 1987.

NGOs and the Law in Central Asia: A Working Conference Co-Sponsored by the American Legal Consortium and Counterpart Consortium. Conference Proceedings. Convened in Issyk-Kul, Kyrgyzstan on 30 Oct.-3 Nov., 1995. Almaty, Kazakhstan: American Legal Consortium, December 1995.

Report on Activities in Democracy, Governance and Participation in the CIS, Central and Eastern Europe. New York: United Nations Development Programme/Regional Directorate for Europe and the CIS, July 1995.

Rutzen, D.B., ed. *Select Legislative Texts and Commentaries on Central and East European Not-for-Profit Law.* Sofia, Bulgaria: International Center for Not-for-Profit Law, European Foundation Centre Orpheus Programme, and Union of Bulgarian Foundations, 1995.

The NGLS Handbook of UN Agencies, Programmes and Funds Working for Economic and Social Development. Geneva: United Nations Non-Governmental Liaison Service, 1994.

Who Helps Children. Moscow: Charities Aid Foundation, 1994 (in Russian).

ARTICLES AND REPORTS

Bivainis, J. "The Legal Regulation of Non-Profit Organisations in Lithuania," Vilnius, April 1995.

Campbell, P. "Institutional Development: Basic Principles and Strategies," Selected Occasional Papers 1986-1990. Geneva: International Council of Voluntary Agencies, 1990, pp. 63-78.

Campbell, P. "Strengthening Organisations," NGO Management, No. 18. Geneva: International Council of Voluntary Agencies, July/Sept. 1990, pp. 21-24.

Covey, J. "Organisation Development and NGOs," NGO Management, No. 10. Geneva: International Council of Voluntary Agencies, July/Sept. 1988, pp. 19-21.

"Danish Assistance to Central & Eastern Europe 1995," Copenhagen: Ministry of Foreign Affairs, June 1995.

Fowler, A. "Building Partnerships Between Northern and Southern Developmental NGOs: Issues for the Nineties," Development in Practice, Vol. 1, No. 1. Oxford, UK: OXFAM, March 1991.

Haruoja, M. "The Role of NGOs in the Management of Migration Issues in the Baltic States," paper presented at the Seminar on Migratory Movements Within, Towards and from Central and Eastern Europe. Strasbourg, France, November 27-29, 1995.

Huntington, R. "Accelerating Institutional Development," PVO Institutional Development Evaluation Series Final Report. Washington DC: United States Agency for International Development, Office of Private and Voluntary Cooperation, September 1987.

"Relations Between Southern and Northern NGOs: Policy Guidelines," revised. International Council of Voluntary Agencies. Geneva: ICVA, March 1990.

Institutional Partnerships Project. Brochure and Fact Sheet. Washington, DC: International Research and Exchanges Board, undated.

"InterAction Situation Report for Private Voluntary Organizations' Current Activities in the Newly Independent States of the Former Soviet Union," Washington, DC: InterAction, December 1994.

"InterAction Situation Report for Private Voluntary Organizations' Current Activities in the Newly Independent States of the Former Soviet Union," Subreport: Caucasus. Washington, DC: InterAction, December, 1994.

Kazakov, O. "The Formation and Trends of Development of the Voluntary Sector in Russia," Working Paper Series: Impediments to Voluntarism. Alexandria, VA: America's Development Foundation and Interlegal, undated.

"Practical Guide for Refugees and Internally Displaced Persons." Tbilisi: Georgian Committee of the Helsinki Citizens' Assembly, 1995 (in Russian).

Quigley, K.F. "For Democracy's Sake: Background Paper," Washington, DC: The Woodrow Wilson Center, 1995. Paper presented to the Bratislava Workshop, November 2-3, 1995 as part of the project, "For Democracy's Sake: Assessing Independent Efforts to Strengthen Democracy in Central Europe 1989-1994."

"Quarterly Activity Report of the Siberian NGO Support Center," Russian Civic Initiatives for Democratic and Economic Reform Program. Yarmouth, ME: Fund Echo Partnership, June 1995.

Salamon, L.M. and Anheier, H.K. "Toward an Understanding of the International Nonprofit Sector," Working Paper Series. Baltimore, MD: The Johns Hopkins Comparative Nonprofit Sector Project, 1992.

Siegel, D. and Yancey, J. "The Rebirth of Civil Society: The Development of the Nonprofit Sector in East Central Europe and the Role of Western Assistance," New York: The Rockefeller Brothers Fund, undated.

"The Citizens Network for Foreign Affairs," Semi-annual Report for the Civic Initiative Program for Democratic and Economic Reform in Russia. Citizens Network, October 1995.

"The Civic Initiatives Program for Democratic and Economic Reform in Russia. Implementation Plan and Budget." Civic Initiatives Program Consortium, April 1995.

PERIODICALS AND NEWSLETTERS

Initiatives in the New Independent States. Quarterly newsletter of the PVO/NIS Project. Washington, DC: World Learning, Inc.

Money and Charity. A magazine published in Russian. Moscow: Charities Aid Foundation.

NGO Law in Brief in the New Independent States. A publication in the periodic series of PVO/NIS Project bulletins. Washington, DC: World Learning, Inc., Winter 1995.

NGO Management. A quarterly newsletter of the NGO Management Network of ICVA. Geneva: International Council of Voluntary Agencies.

New Georgia. Monthly newsletter for NGOs in the Republic of Georgia. Tbilisi: Published cooperatively by ISAR and ITIC.

DIRECTORIES

Address List of OSCE Missions. Washington, DC: Commission on Security and Cooperation in Europe, February, 1996.

Channels: A Guide to Third Sector Projects, Organizations and Work Opportunities in the New Independent States. Seattle, WA: Center for Civil Society International, 1995.

Directory of Private Voluntary Non-Governmental and International Organizations Delivering Humanitarian Aid to Refugees, the Internally Displaced and Vulnerable People in Azerbaijan. Baku, Azerbaijan: Save the Children, March 1996.

Eurasia Foundation Grants Listing: Grants to Support Development of the Nongovernmental Sector in the NIS. Washington, DC: Eurasia Foundation, January 1996.

List of NGOs in Central Asia. Washington, DC: World Learning, Inc., 1996.

Membership Directory of the Estonian Foundation Centre. Tallinn: Eesti Fondide Keskus (Estonian Foundation Centre), 1995.

PVO/NIS Subgrantee Projects List. Projects in International Development and Training. Washington, DC: World Learning, Inc., 1996.

Survey of NGOs in Georgia. Tbilisi: Open Society Georgia Foundation, December 1995.

U.S.-Baltic Partnerships. Washington, DC: U.S.-Baltic Foundation, undated.

Who's Who in Armenian NGOs. Washington, DC and Yerevan: NGO Training and Resource Center of the Armenian Assembly of America, 1996.

World Bank NGO Database for the CIS and East and Central Europe - Environment Web. Washington, DC: The World Bank, 1996.

World Bank NGO Database for the CIS and East and Central Europe - Operations Policy Department. Washington, DC: The World Bank, 1996.

Appendix IV: Legal Analysis of Legislation Concerning NGOs

The historic changes taking place in the former Soviet Union include the development of a fledgling NGO sector.[1] During Soviet times, civil society was largely suppressed. As the state controlled virtually every aspect of society, there was no need for laws governing NGOs. In 1991, at the end of the period of *glasnost*, a law "On Public Associations" took effect in the Soviet Union. This law, progressive at the time, is still the model for most laws governing not-for-profit organizations in the former Soviet states. Along with new political systems and market economies, a strong, diverse non-profit sector is emerging as well. To encourage and regulate these organizations, new laws are needed. Below is an overview of the status of such laws, and suggestions for their reform.

International Norms and Ideals

NGOs are a fundamental part of civil society. Among their many benefits are contributions to pluralism, support for democratic institutions, social stability and the rule of law, economic prosperity in a market economy, and social well-being.[2] NGOs can provide services which the government cannot afford to provide, and address issues which are difficult for the government to pursue. Laws are a means of institutionalizing these benefits. While certain general legal principles are accepted internationally, some provisions can be modified to reflect local social, economic, and political customs.

Some basic concepts are important in evaluating a country's NGO laws.[3] For instance, it is critical that the laws be transparent. They should protect internationally recognized rights to free speech, association, and assembly. Laws should allow for the existence of NGOs as independent, autonomous juridical entities. Freedom of association requires that informal organizations also be free to operate, while having the option of registration to receive certain tax and other legal benefits. The laws should state all rights necessary to NGOs' accomplishment of their goals. And they should provide for the protection of individuals, while allowing for government oversight to prevent fraud or danger to the public interest. The laws should be general, objective, non-arbitrary, and reviewable by an independent judiciary.

Substantively, all rules—general and fiscal—should be clear and simple. Registration should be not only optional, but expeditious as well. Non-governmental organizations' duties should be plainly established, and proportional to any benefits (such as tax-exempt status) conferred by the state. An NGO should be allowed to have a bank account in its own name, communicate through all media, engage in standard legal transactions, and otherwise fulfill its goals.

Legal forms such as foundations and associations might also be distinguished. Laws may state purposes for which an NGO can be formed, while providing flexibility for new ideas. The scope of NGO activity should be broadly defined, and any restrictions, such as those on political or business activities, should be precisely and narrowly delineated. And fiscal rules should include clear criteria for income/profit, property, transfer, sales, and other tax exemptions for NGOs, as well as deductions for those making donations and grants.

Organizational structure should be legislated clearly and concisely. Laws can specify requirements for registration, fees, founders, and members, powers of the organization, voting, governance and dissolution. In exchange for NGOs' receiving government benefits such as tax-exempt status or the right to solicit funds from the public, laws may impose detailed requirements for reports and records, to encourage public disclosure, accountability and confidence, while not becoming overly burdensome to the organization. The operation of foreign organizations should also be addressed.

Finally, it is critical for laws to be easily administered. There must be a practical balance between simplicity of concept and clarity of detail. This ease of understanding facilitates the productive growth and operation of the NGO sector, by making easier both NGO compliance and government enforcement.

The Range of NGO Laws in the fSU

Since their independence, all of the former Soviet republics have drafted or passed new laws, or amendments to old ones, governing the formation and regulation of non-governmental organizations. The quantity of revisions varies greatly: some countries have made small adjustments, while others have developed a whole range of statutes regarding different types of organizations, as well as tax laws, new constitutional provisions, and various regulations and presidential decrees. In general form, substance, and practice, there are still many similarities among the laws of the countries of the fSU. It is in the details that the differences become apparent.

In most countries of the former Soviet Union, NGOs are governed by laws covering the broader category of "public associations," which are usually defined as not-for-profit, and can be created and/or funded by the state as well as the private sector. Sometimes terminology such as "not-for-profit association" or "non-commercial organization" is used in addition or as an alternative. Whatever name is used, the basic legislation generally takes the same form.

Most legislation on public associations starts with a description of the purpose of the law and the types of organizations, in form and substance, that it covers. Ukraine's law is fairly typical in its delineation of the purposes of and limitations on NGOs. A citizens' association is defined as a "voluntary [NGO] founded on the base of common interests for the joint exercise of civil rights and freedoms," formed to pursue and protect "citizens' lawful social, economic, creative, age, cultural, sport, and other common interests," such as scientific and educational ones.[4] Prohibited are "organizations that aim to change the constitutional system, undermine national security, propagandize about war, or ignite national strife and racial discrimination."[5] Some countries' laws on public associations govern political parties, trade unions, and/or religious organizations, while other countries distinguish such groups under separate legislative provisions.

Legislation then usually discusses the formation of an NGO, its internal governance and membership, its charter, registration, rights and obligations, property, sources of revenue, business activity, state protection and oversight, liability for violations of law, international contacts, and termination. The laws vary in the degree of detail with which they describe requirements for the above, and in the extent to which they provide for such things as appeal of government decisions to courts.

In the former Soviet states, tax laws and civil codes must also be consulted for provisions applicable to NGOs. Constitutions generally, and statutes sometimes, guarantee freedom of association and dissemination of ideas. Statutes sometimes refer to the Universal Declaration of Human Rights, while containing many restrictions on these freedoms. Presidential decrees, statements of national ministries, and local regulations are also factors.

All of these laws change frequently, and there is rarely a uniform process for their publication. These factors often lead to inconsistencies among laws, confusion as to which take precedence, and extreme difficulty in finding the laws at all. As discussed below, this lack of transparency hinders compliance and leaves wide gaps for arbitrary and inconsistent enforcement.

Some Problematic Laws

The fast pace of legal reform, new political systems, much information from outside, and eagerness to solidify independence, has lead to a proliferation of related, overlapping, contradictory, hard to find, and frequently changing laws. This makes both enforcement and compliance difficult. An increase in regulation can bring greater clarity to rights and duties, as well as more confusion, bureaucracy, and arbitrary enforcement. A statute filled with clear, progressive parameters for NGO operation can be rendered fragile by restrictions on NGO establishment which are open to unbounded interpretation by the government. In Azerbaijan, for example, the law allows free dissemination of information about an organization's goals,[6] yet prohibits political objectives or those which encroach on public morals.[7] It is not difficult to imagine an NGO purpose which could be characterized in this fashion.

Throughout the world, NGOs function under frequently burdensome and bureaucratic laws. Both their substance and implementation determine the effect of these laws on NGO operations. Accordingly, the following is not intended as an exhaustive analysis of NGO laws in the fSU. It is, rather, an overview of some of the legal difficulties faced by NGOs there. The examples presented are not necessarily exclusive to the countries from which they are taken. They are simply illustrative, and should provide a framework for both operating in the region and identifying potential areas of reform.

Registration

Registration is one of the most inscrutable areas of NGO law in the former Soviet Union. Despite the internationally recognized right to freedom of association, most states of the fSU require NGOs to register with the government to become a "legal person" or "legal entity." Most laws do not make clear the legal status of an unregistered NGO, or whether or under what conditions such an organization may operate. There are some noteworthy exceptions. Russia's new Federal Law on Public Associations explicitly acknowledges a public association's right to organize and function without prior government approval or registration.[8] Estonia's law states that unregistered NGOs are not legal entities "and shall be subject to provisions regulating "societies.""[9] The law also outlines liabilities for transactions carried out by such organizations.[10] A few laws prohibit "secret associations," without defining this term. Basic questions of implementation and interpretation are raised by the use of such vague terms. For example, does this prohibit a meeting or group of any type of which the government is not informed or to which it is not invited?

The dubious requirement of registration is complicated by laws that make the process time-consuming, expensive, incomprehensible, and otherwise difficult to comply with. Initially, most countries require a minimum number of natural or legal persons to form an organization, thus eliminating the legitimate functioning of the simplest grassroots "organization:" an individual laboring at his or her favorite cause. Some countries require a small number of founders. Estonia, for instance, requires two natural or legal persons,[11] and Russia, where registration is still necessary for recognition as a legal entity, requires three natural persons.[12] Several Central Asian republics[13] and Belarus[14] require an unwieldy 10, and Georgia mandates an unworkable minimum of 50.[15]

Upon meeting this basic requirement, organizations in states of the fSU must then file numerous documents with the registering authorities. Preparation is often very time-consuming, difficult, and expensive. One must identify what documents are required, where to file them, and by what procedure; draft or collect the appropriate documents, and have them translated (sometimes into two languages), notarized, and photocopied.

The basic registration document is the charter, or by-laws, of an organization. This is usually drafted at an initial meeting of founders, and its contents, as prescribed by statute, ordinarily include the association's name and form; address; territory of operation; goals and objectives, and methods of their achievement; criteria for membership and dismissal; rights and obligations of members; formation procedure, powers, and terms of office of managing bodies; sources of funds and assets; and procedures for changing or amending the charter, auditing, reorganization, and termination.

Heavy bureaucratic burdens often encumber the registration process. Many documents are often required, and some requirements are left to the discretion of registering authorities. Registration fees are often extremely high or unspecified, also to be determined by the registering authority at the time of application. Such discretion can result in frequent and arbitrary rule changes, increasing the difficulty of compliance. Organizations must often register with both national and regional authorities. And this complex procedure must often be repeated when amending or changing a charter.

The government generally has as much as two or three months in which to respond to registration applications, and has broad discretion as to whether to accept, reject, or postpone consideration of the application. Reasons for rejection range from substantive to technical, and specific to general, problems with documents. There is no provision for interim modification of documents, which could reduce rejections. For instance, minor technicalities such as an applicant attempting to register under a name already taken by another organization, could be easily rectified. With a central, publicly accessible list of registered NGOs, both applicants and registering agencies could check and fix this problem immediately, rather than waiting two or three months for outright rejection. In addition, some states have a long and general list of permissible reasons for rejection that could be interpreted to include almost anything. For example, Moldova's law allows rejection if there is "uncertain information" in the papers, or if the name of the organization "insults morals, and national and religious feelings of citizens."[16] Further, consideration of the application can be postponed for up to three months due to anything that "breaks" this law.[17]

Some laws require reasons for rejection to be given in writing within a short period of time after the decision is made, and some allow for an NGO to appeal the government's decision in court—although some do not. Even where an appeal is allowed, one must take into consideration the varying stages of development of independent judiciaries in the fSU. Whether or not any of these procedures are in place, a rejected application seems to require an NGO to start the process anew, costing it tremendous resources, both time and money, which it frequently does not have. These hurdles can be a great deterrent for any organization hoping to function in this system.

For the registration application of international NGOs, some countries require documentation from a landlord confirming that it will allow use of its premises as the organization's legal address. Finding an office can be time consuming and difficult, and is a premature burden for both parties—an NGO not yet sure if or when it will be allowed to work in the region, and a potential landlord asked to keep space available under such circumstances.

Tax

Tax rates in the former Soviet Union are generally very high, and there are very few reduced rates or exemptions for not-for-profit organizations. The existing tax benefits, as well as deductions for donors, are rarely significant. Some countries do not allow NGOs to engage in any commercial activity, even if it is related to the organization's purpose. In light of the limited funds generally possessed by NGOs, these factors combine to create tremendous financial difficulties for these groups. Some laws provide broader or total exemptions for international NGOs.

The tax laws are often confusing. Profit, income, property and value-added tax laws rarely make general distinctions between NGOs and business or commercial enterprises. Reduced rates and exemptions are frequently based not on the distinctive nature of NGOs, but on selected categories of organizational purpose, or the source and/or use of certain funds, and are even designated for individual organizations. Tax benefits are likely to be given to government-supported associations, whose public benefit, form, and purpose resemble independent NGOs; these organizations are sometimes referred to as quasi-NGOs (QUANGOs) or government-organized NGOs (GONGOs).

Tax benefits are commonly granted to associations for disabled persons, veterans, women, youth, and the environment, among others. Uzbekistan, for example, exempts from its profit tax, in addition to many of the above, such organizations as enterprises which receive profits from the restoration of historical and cultural monuments, and training enterprises and organizations, as well as the Red Crescent Society and the Association of the Culture of Uzbekistan.[18] And benefits are not always distributed evenly; one group might be exempt from property taxes, while another might have certain income tax deductions. Specific organizations are often designated for exemption as well.

Sources of revenue also affect certain tax benefits. Several countries exempt from income or profit tax those organizations which receive their money solely from membership dues, donations and the like; that is, they do not engage in commercial activity. Others might exempt membership dues, for instance, while taxing grants. Some allow non-commercial organizations to engage in commercial activity. A few of those tax all income from such endeavors, and some only tax income from commercial activity that is not related to the organization's charter purpose. Some countries also reduce the tax rate for income from activities related to such things as education, medicine, sports training, and publishing.

Laws occasionally allow deductions for donations and other uses of funds. Businesses giving donations to non-profit organizations might get a tax deduction, but often only up to one or two percent of their income.

Many other aspects of the fSU's tax laws are complicated by their generality or by their detail, by terminology not clearly defined, and by rules which appear in many different codes. It is not unusual for a presidential decree to clarify or change a statutory provision, while taxpayers receive delayed or no knowledge of the new rule. And sometimes tax laws are stated in legislation other than tax codes. For example, in Kyrgyzstan, while the "Law on Foreign Investments" states that the republic's general tax legislation governs foreign investors,[19] it contains considerable detail on tax benefits for that group.[20]

Government Oversight

Another common aspect of fSU law is the tremendous amount of government oversight of NGOs. Even when NGOs are given broad mandates as to their freedom of operation, the time spent in complying with legal obligations and reporting on this compliance is a tremendous burden. Laws often spell out in great detail the operating procedures of NGOs. On the other hand, as is often the case, some requirements or prohibitions are so general as to be open to broad interpretation by the government, thus creating a compliance quagmire for the organization. Enforcement of these extensive rules can entail government involvement in NGO activity. And reporting requirements are usually burdensome.

Another means of government control of NGOs is its ability to dissolve organizations. Laws give many bases for involuntary dissolution of NGOs. Sometimes there is no provision for appeal to the courts; even when there is, an NGO is at least temporarily deprived of its ability to function, and incurs the time and expense of appealing and then, if successful, possibly re-registering.

Legislating details of NGO operating procedure go as far as Estonia's law, which spells out how to decide what may be discussed at a meeting, and different percentages of votes needed for various internal resolutions.[21] Latvia calls for limitless reporting requirements; numerous government departments can *each* audit an organization's financial and operational activities *at least* once every two years.[22] It also prohibits a participant's withdrawal of its "investment shares" within two years of joining the organization.[23] A number of countries explicitly allow officials of supervising government agencies to attend all NGO activities, and to request documentation—and explanations—of all decisions made by the organization. If such agencies find violations of the law or charter, they might temporarily suspend an organization's operations or begin dissolution proceedings. While such decisions may be appealable in court, they have an immediate chilling effect on the NGO's work. Also, one must question the significance of such appeals in countries which have not yet developed a truly independent judiciary.

In practice, government authorities are almost unlimited in their ability to terminate an NGO's existence. With so many requirements in hard-to-find statutes and decrees, it is easy for a grassroots organization, with little, if any, legal experience or understanding, to overlook any such detail in its daily operations. And again, it is difficult to determine strict compliance when any "interested person" can seek involuntary dissolution because an NGO's purpose or operations are "inconsistent with *good practice*" (emphasis added).[24]

Prospects for Reform

International norms provide a framework for reform of NGO laws in the fSU. Examples for incorporating these norms into local culture might be found in the experience of some countries of Eastern Europe, which have similar political and economic histories, and which embarked on a similar reform process a few years earlier than the former Soviet states.

With all of the rapid change within the fSU itself, there are emerging some examples of progress in NGO legal development. Russia, for instance, enacted a new law on public associations in 1995,[25] and its public announcement and dissemination of that law was in and of itself a positive step toward transparency and effective NGO operation. Among the encouraging provisions in the new Russian law are those that provide for a constructive relationship between the government and NGOs. For example, NGOs may perform work and render services under contract with the federal government.[26] And among the fundamental rights of public associations, as stated in the law, are the ability to represent and protect the rights of all citizens before state and local governments, and to submit proposals to and participate in decision-making with government bodies.[27] Unfortunately, the exercise of these and other rights, such as information distribution and organization of rallies, can be restricted with respect to "public associations created by foreign citizens and persons without citizenship or with their participation."[28]

Lithuania, which has made much progress in the development of a broad range of laws governing NGOs, has two central compilations of laws. The Computer Information Department of the Seimas (parliament) Chancellery coordinates a legislative database, and the Ministry of Justice's Legal Information Centre oversees a register containing all laws, decrees, resolutions and other related documents.[29] Public access to such information represents an important step toward transparency and ease of administration.

Moldovan law gives citizens the power to bring a judicial or administrative action against acts, by the state or its officials, which "hamper the foundation of public associations of citizens and the realization of their legal and charter activity."[30] The law also states specific remedies.[31]

In some countries, ideas for cooperation are being discussed between the traditionally adversarial groups of NGO leaders and government officials. In the autumn of 1995, government and NGO representatives from all five Central Asian republics met to discuss their points of view on various issues and prospects for reform. They developed some concrete ideas for cooperation in these endeavors.[32] NGOs in Estonia have also had meetings and established a dialogue with officials from different branches of government.[33]

International NGOs can play a useful role in the development of the NGO sectors of the fSU. Local NGOs in the region, while relatively inexperienced in legal and management details, are often very dedicated, with significant knowledge of issues and their relation to local applications. They have a great understanding of their society, and the parameters of political, economic, and social realities. To this, international organizations can contribute experience with logistics, organization, and finance, as well as legal compliance and effective NGO-government cooperation. They can also provide assistance in critical networking and coordination among local and international NGOs.

All of the above illustrates the tremendous importance of a viable NGO sector, supported by the rule of law. Active and open NGOs, operating in conjunction with the government under clear and easily administrable laws, are a vital component of a free and functional civil society. In the legal and social development of the states of the former Soviet Union, the continued participation of local and international NGOs is critical. Their contribution to legislative reform can ensure further progress in this rapidly changing region.

Notes

1. The term NGO is used herein to refer to the generally accepted concept of a non-governmental, not-for-profit organization which provides public benefits. As the text of this report makes clear, in the fSU local NGO activities sometimes include entrepreneurial activities.

2. "Blueprints Project: Issues to Consider in Drafting Laws Governing Not-for-Profit Organizations," International Center for Not-for-Profit Law.

3. Many of the following international norms and ideals are based on concepts developed in the Blueprints Project, id.

4. "NGOs and NGO Law in Ukraine," Vyatcheslav Zhilikov, in "NGO Law in Brief in the New Independent States," Forum 1, Winter 1995, by World Learning Inc., p. 23.

5. Id.

6. Zakon azerbaidzhanskoi respubliki ob obshchstvennykh ob'edineniiakh [Law on Public Associations], 10 November 1992, Article 8.

7. Id. at Article 4.

8. Federal'nyi zakon ob obshchstvennykh ob'edineniiakh [Federal Law on Public Associations], 19 May 1995, no. 82-FZ , Article 3.

9. Law on Not-For-Profit Associations, 1 April 1996, Section 2(2).

10. Id. at Section 13.

11. Id. at Section 6.

12. Federal'nyi zakon ob obshchstvennykh ob'edineniiakh [Federal Law on Public Associations], 19 May 1995, no. 82-FZ , Article 18.

13. Zakon Respubliki Kyrgyzstan ob obshchestvennykh ob'edineniiakh [Law on Public Associations], 1 February 1991, no. 359-XII, Article 8; Zakon Tadzhikskoi Sovetskoi Sotsialisticheskoi Respubliki ob obshchstvennykh ob'edineniiakh v Tadzhikskoi SSR [Law on Public Associations of the Tajik SSR], 12 December 1990, no. 171, as amended 14 March 1992, Article 9; and Zakon Respubliki Uzbekistan ob obshchestvennykh ob'edineniiakh v Respublike Uzbekistan [Law on Public Associations], 15 February 1991, no. 223-XII, as amended 3 June 1992, Article 8. In Kazakhstan, the Public Associations Law also requires 10 natural persons to found an NGO (Zakon Kazakhskoi Sovetskoi Sotsialisticheskoi Respubliki ob obshchstvennykh ob'edineniiakh v Kazakhskoi SSR [Law on Public Associations of the Kazakh SSR], 27 June 1991, Article 10), while the more recently adopted Civil Code states that "[a] legal entity may be established by one or several founders," (Grazhdanskii kodeks Respubliki Kazakhstan [Civil Code of the Republic of Kazakhstan], 1995, Article 40(1)). On 4 April 1996, the Kazakhstan Parliament reportedly passed a new law governing NGOs. The president has apparently not yet signed this law, and no further information is currently available. It is possible that the new law will reconcile this inconsistency.

14. Zakon ob obshchstvennykh ob'edineniiakh [Law on Public Associations], 4 October 1994, Article 8.

15. Zakon Respubliki Gruziia ob obshchstvennykh ob'edineniiakh grazhdan [Law of the Republic of Georgia on Public Associations of Citizens], 14 June 1994, Article 10.

16. Law of the Republic of Moldova on Public Associations, 1995, Article 26.

17. Id. at Articles 22 & 25.

18. Instructions of the Ministry of Finance and State Taxation Committee of the Republic of Uzbekistan, "On Order of Evaluation and Payment of Profit [Income] Tax Into the State Budget by Enterprises and Organizations," no. 170, 22 December 1994, Article 18.

19. Zakon ob inostrannykh investitsiiakh v Respublike Kyrgyzstan [Law on Foreign Investment in the Republic of Kyrgyzstan], 28 June 1991, no. 536, Article 19.

20. Id. at Articles 20, 21, & 22.

21. Law on Not-For-Profit Associations, 1 April 1996, Chapter 4.

22. Law on Not-for-Profit Organizations, 17 December 1991; amended 11 May 1993, Article 12.

23. Id. at Article 10.

24. Law on Not-For-Profit Associations (Estonia), 1 April 1996, Section 42.

25. Federalinyi zakon ob obshchstvennykh obiedineniiakh [Federal Law on Public Associations], 19 May 1995, no. 82-FZ.

26. Id. at Article 17.

27. Id. at Article 27.

28. Id.

29. "The Legal Regulation of Non-Profit Organizations in Lithuania," Juozas Bivainis, April 1995.

30. Law of the Republic of Moldova on Public Associations, 1995, Article 13(1).

31. Id. at Article 13(2).

32. "NGOs and the Law in Central Asia, A Working Conference" Co-sponsored by The American Legal Consortium and Counterpart Consortium, supported by USAID, at Issyk-kul, Kyrgyzstan, 30 October-1November 1995.

33. Report on Legal and Legislative Developments for the NFPOs in Estonia, by Rita Tamm, Executive Director, Estonian Foundation Centre.

Appendix V: Laws Pertaining to NGOs in the fSU

This is a list of laws that concern the work of NGOs in the former Soviet Union. The provisions of the laws listed may affect the establishment or operation of NGOs in the region. Because laws change often, the Open Society Institute cannot guarantee that the list is complete or up-to-date. To facilitate research, the titles of the laws are provided, whenever possible, in Russian (transliterated) when there is a Russian version. Translations of the titles into English are placed between brackets.

AZERBAIJAN
Zakon azerbaidzhanskoi respubliki ob obshchstvennykh ob'edineniiakh [Law on Public Associations], 10 November 1992

ARMENIA
[Decree of the Presidium of the Supreme Soviet of the Armenian SSR on Current Rules for the Registration of Civil Associations], 30 October 1989

BELARUS
Grazhdanskii kodeks respubliki Belarusi [Civil Code of Belarus], Arts. 24-39 (formation, activity, and dissolution of legal entities)

Zakon ob obshchstvennykh ob'edineniiakh [Law on Public Associations], 4 October 1994

Zakon Respubliki Belarusi o nalogakh na dokhody i pribyl' predpriiatii, ob'edinenii, organizatsii [Law on the Taxation of the Income and Profit of Enterprises, Associations, and Institutions]

O naloge na pribyli [Regulation on the Taxation of Profits], 1 January 1995, no. 742/12

Pis'mo Ministerstva Finansov Respubliki Belarusi-Ligoty po nalogooblozheniiu [Letter of the Ministry of Finance of Belarus on Tax Privileges], 23 February 1993, no. 13-02/536

Glavnaia gosudarstvennaia nalogovaia inspektsiia pri kabinete ministrov respubliki Belarus' - o naloge na pribyl' [Clarification of the Regulation on the Taxation of Profits], 29 September 1995, no. 02/158 [Rules for the Registration of Public Associations], 15 May 1995, no. 108

Glavnaia gosudarstvennaia nalogovaia inspektsiia pri kabinete ministrov respubliki Belarus'- o vnesenii izmenenii v metodicheskie ukazaniia ot 17 ianvaria 1994 goda N. 16 "O poriadke ischisleniia naloga na pribyl' " [Changes in Regulation of Taxation], 27 April 1995, no. 02/73

ESTONIA
[Law on Not-For-Profit Associations], 1 April 1996

[Law on Foundations], 1 August 1995

[Income Tax Law], 1 January 1994, as amended 15 March 1994

[Law on Taxation], 6 January 1994

GEORGIA
Zakon Respubliki Gruziia ob obshchstvennykh ob'edineniiakh grazhdan [Law of the Republic of Georgia on Public Associations of Citizens], 14 June 1994

KAZAKHSTAN
Konstitutsiia Respubliki Kazakhstan [Constitution of the Republic of Kazakhstan], 1995, Article 23 (freedom of association)

Grazhdanskii kodeks Respubliki Kazakhstan [Civil Code of the Republic of Kazakhstan], 1995, Arts. 33 to 51 (creation, activities and dissolution of legal entities), and Arts. 106 to 110 (types of public associations, including religious associations)

Zakon Kazakhskoi Sovetskoi Sotsialisticheskoi Respubliki ob obshchstvennykh ob'edineniiakh v Kazakhskoi SSR [Law on Public Associations of the Kazakh SSR], 27 June 1991

Ugolovnyi kodeks Kazakhskoi SSR [Criminal Code of the Kazakh SSR], Arts. 63-3

Ukaz Presidenta Respubliki Kazakhstan o nalogooblozhenii pribyli i dokhodov predpriiatii [Decree of the President of the Republic of Kazakhstan on the Taxation of the Profits and the Income of Enterprises], 22 February 1994

Ukaz Presidenta Respubliki Kazakhstan, imeioshchii silu Zakona, o gosu-darstvennoi registratsii iuridicheskikh lits [Decree of the President of the

Republic of Kazakhstan on State Registration of Legal Entities], 17 April 1995, no. 2198

Ukaz Presidenta Respubliki Kazakhstan, imeioshchii silu Zakona, o vnesenii izmenenii i dopolnenii v nekotorye zakonodatel'nye akty Respubliki Kazakhstan, i ukaz presidenta Respubliki Kazakhstan, imeioshchii silu Zakona, "o gosudarstvennoi registratsii iuridicheskikh lits" [Decree of the President of the Republic of Kazakhstan about Modifications and Additions to Several Statutory Instruments of the Republic of Kazakhstan and to the Decree of the President of the Republic of Kazakhstan on State Registration of Legal Entities], 19 October 1995

Dopolneniia sviazannye s Ukazom Presidenta Respubliki Kazakhstan ot 19 oktiabria 1995 goda [Additions related to the Decree of the President of Kazakhstan dated 19 October 1995]

Ukaz Prezidiuma Verkhovnogo Soveta SSSR o poriadke organizatsii i provedeniia mitingov shestvii i demonstratsii v SSSR [Decree of the Presidium of the Supreme Soviet of the USSR on the Procedure for the Organization and the Conduct of Meetings, Marches and Demonstrations in the USSR], 28 July 1989

Reshenie ispolnitel'nogo komiteta Almatinskogo gorodskogo soveta narodnikh deputatov o meste provedeniia mitingov, demonstratsii [Decision of the Executive Committee of the Almaty Soviet of People's Deputies regarding the Venue for Political Meetings and Demonstrations], 5 February 1990, no. 4/37

Polozhenie ministra iustitsii Respubliki Kazakhstan o poriadke gosudarstvennoi registratsii iuridicheskikh lits organami ministerstva iustitsii Respubliki Kazakhstan [Regulation of the Minister of Justice of the Republic of Kazakhstan on the Procedure for State Registration of Legal Entities with the Bodies of the Ministry of Justice of the Republic of Kazakhstan], 14 July 1995

N.B. On 4 April 1996, Kazakhstan's Parliament adopted a new Law on Public Associations defining the rights and permitted activities of public associations. No further details are yet available.

KYRGYZSTAN

Konstitutsiia Kyrgyzskoi Respubliki [Constitution of the Kyrgyz Republic], 5 May 1993, Article 16 (freedom of association)

Zakon Respubliki Kyrgyzstan ob obshchestvennykh ob'edineniiakh [Law on Public Associations], 1 February 1991, no. 359-XII

Grazhdanskii kodeks respubliki Kyrgyzstan [Civil Code of Kyrgyzstan], 1992, Arts. 27 to 41 (formation, activity, and dissolution of legal entities), Arts. 100 to 105 (property of public organizations)

Zakon ob inostrannykh investitsiiakh v Respublike Kyrgyzstan [Law on Foreign Investment in the Republic of Kyrgyzstan], 28 June 1991, no. 536

Pis'mo Gosudarstvennoi nalogovoi inspektsiia pri ministerstve finansov Kyrgyzskoi Respubliki [Clarification Regarding the Taxation (Social Security) of Public Associations in Kyrgyzstan], 18 December 1995

Pis'mo gosudarstvennoi nalogoi inspektsii Kyrgyzskoi Respubliki [Letter of the Government Tax Inspection Board of the Republic of Kyrgyzstan], 28 April 1994, no. 06-07/55 (social security tax)

LATVIA

[Law on Not-for-Profit Organizations], 17 December 1991; as amended 11 May 1993

[Law on the Income of Entreprises], Arts. 20 and 21

LITHUANIA

[Law on Community Organizations], 1995

[Draft Law on Associations], approved by the Government 1995

[Draft Law on Foundations], approved by the Government 1995

[Law on Charitable Assistance and Aid], 1993

MOLDOVA

[Law of the Republic of Moldova on Public Associations], 1995

Russia

Konstitutsiia Rossiskoi Federatsii [Constitution of the Russian Federation], 12 December 1993, Article 30 (freedom of association)

Grazhdanskii kodeks Rossiskoi Federatsii [Civil Code of the Russian Federation], 1 January 1995, Part 1, chapter IV, Arts. 48 and 50

Federal'nyi zakon ob obshchstvennykh ob'edineniiakh [Federal Law on Public Associations], 19 May 1995, no. 82-FZ

Prikaz Ministerstva iustitsii Rossiskoi Federatsii ob utverzhdenii v novoi redaktsii pravil registratsii ustavov (polozhenii) religioznykh ob'edinenii [Order of the Ministry of Justice of the Russian Federation Approving the New Version of the Rules for the Registration of the By-Laws of Religious Organizations], 30 November 1994, no. 19-01-159-94

Federal'nyi zakon o blagotvoritel'noi deiatel'nosti i blagotvoritel'nikh organizatsiiakh [Federal Law on Charitable Activity and Charitable Organizations], 11 August 1995, no. 135-FZ

Prikaz Ministerstva iustitsii Rossiskoi Federatsii ob utverzhdenii novoi redaktsii Vremennikh pravil registratsii ustavov politicheskikh partii i inykh obshchestvennykh ob'edinenii v Ministerstve iustitsii Rossiskoi Federatsii [Order of the Ministry of Justice of the Russian Federation Approving the Rules for the Registration of the By-Laws of Political Parties and Other Public Associations with the Ministry of Justice of the Russian Federation], 16 September 1994, no. 19-47-94-94

Federal'nyi zakon o nekommercheskikh organizatsiiakh [Law on Non-Commercial Organizations], 12 January 1996, no. 7-FZ

Zakon goroda Moskvy o blagotvoritel'noi deiatel'nosti [Law of the City of Moscow on Charitable Activity], 5 July 1995, no. 11-46

Rasporiazhenie mera Moskvy ob utverzhdenii polozheniia o poriadke registratsii nekommercheskikh organizatsii v gorode Moskve [Order of the Mayor Of Moscow Approving the Regulation on the Procedure for Registration of Non-Commercial Organizations in Moscow], 29 December 1992, no. 598-RM, as amended 8 November 1993 and 7 December 1994

TAJIKISTAN
Konstitutsiia Respubliki Tadzhikistan [Constitution of the Republic of Tajikistan], Arts. 28 and 29 (freedom of association)

Zakon Tadzhikskoi Sovetskoi Sotsialisticheskoi Respubliki ob obshchest vennykh ob'edineniiakh v Tadzhikskoi SSR [Law on Public Associations of the Tajik SSR], 12 December 1990, no. 171, as amended 14 March 1992

Zakon Respubliki Tadzhikistan o vnesenii izmenenii i dopolnenii v Zakon Respubliki Tadzhikistan ob obshchestvennykh ob'edineniiakh v respublike Tadzhikistan [Law of the Republic of Tajikistan on the Introduction of Changes and Additions to the Law of the Republic of Tajikistan on Public Associations in the Republic of Tajikistan], 14 March 1992, no. 600

Zakon Respubliki Tadzhikistan ob inostrannykh investitsiiakh v Respublike Tadzhikistan [Law of the Republic of Tajikistan on Foreign Investments in the Republic of Tajikistan], 10 March 1992

Pravila rassmotrenia zaiavlenii o registratsii ustavov respublikanskikh zven'ev obshchesoiuznykh obshchestvennykh ob'edinenii, a takzhe mezhdunarodnykh, mezhrespublikanskikh, respublikanskikh i mestnykh obshchestvennykh ob'edinenii, deistvuiushchikh v Tadzhikskoi SSR [Rules of Registration of By-Laws of Republican Branches of All-Union Public Associations, as well as International, Inter-Republic, Republic and Local Public Associations, Which Are Active in the Tajik SSR], 28 February 1991, no. 45

TURKMENISTAN
Konstitutsiia Turkmenistana [Constitution of Turkmenistan], 1992, Arts. 27 and 28 (freedom of association)

Zakon Turkmenistana ob obshchestvennykh ob'edineniiakh v Turkmenistane [Law on Public Associations], 1 April 1992

Ukaz Presidenta Turkmenistana o dopolnitel'nykh l'gotakh obshchestvennym organizatsiiam invalidov i ikh chlenam [Decree on Additional Advantages to the Public Associations of Handicapped Persons and their Members], 11 March 1993

Postanovlenie Presidenta Turkmenistana - Voprosy registratsii obshchetvennykh ob'edinenii [Decree of the President of Turkmenistan on Questions of Registration of Public Associations], 3 March 1992, no. 632

Utverzhdeny postanovleniem Presidenta Turkmenistana o pravilakh registratsii obshchestvennykh ob'edinenii ot 3 marta 1992, N. 632 [Approbation of the Decree of the President of Trukmenistan on the Rules for the Registration of Public Associations], 3 March 1992, no. 632

UKRAINE
[Law on Associations of Citizens], 16 June 1992, as amended

UZBEKISTAN
Konstitutsiia Respubliki Uzbekistan [Constitution of the Republic of Uzbekistan], 1992, Arts. 33 and 34 (freedom of association)

Zakon Respubliki Uzbekistan ob obshchestvennykh ob'edineniiakh v Respublike Uzbekistan [Law on Public Associations], 15 February 1991, no. 223-XII, as amended 3 June 1992

Zakon Respubliki Uzbekistan o vnesenii izmenenii i dopolnitelnenii v Zakon Respubliki Uzbekistan ob obshchestvennykh ob'edineniiakh v Respublike Uzbekistan [Law of the Republic of Uzbekistan on the Introduction of Changes and Additions to the Law of the Republic of Uzbekistan on Public Associations in the Republic of Uzbekistan], 3 July 1992, no. 664-XII

Postanovlenie gosudarstvennogo nalogogo komiteta ministerstva finansov Respubliki Uzbekistan o nekotorykh izmeneniiakh poriadka nalogooblozheni-ia dlia otdel'nykh predpriiatii [Regulation of the State Committee on Taxation of the Ministry of Finance of Uzbekistan on Certain Changes in the Method of Taxation of Particular Enterprises], 11 April 1994

Postanovlenie gosudarstvennogo nalogogo komiteta ministerstva finansov Respubliki Uzbekistan o nekotorykh izmeneniiakh poriadka nalogooblozheni-ia v 1995 godu [Regulation of the State Committee on Taxation of the Ministry of Finance of Uzbekistan on Certain Changes in the Method of Taxation for 1995], 3 January 1995

Postanovlenie kabineta ministrov Respubliki Uzbekistan ob uporiadochenii registratsii ustavov obshchestvennykh ob'edinenii v Respublike Uzbekistan

[Regulation of the Cabinet of Ministers of the Republic of Uzbekistan on the Putting in Order of the Registration of By-Laws of Public Associations in the Republic of Kazakhstan], 12 March 1993, no. 132

Utverzhdeny postanovleniem kabineta ministrov ot 12 marta 1993, N. 132-Pravila rassmotreniia zaiavlenii o registratsii ustavov obshchestvennykh ob'edinenii, deistvuiushchikh na territorii Respubliki Uzbekistan [Approbation of the Regulation of the Cabinet of Ministers dated 12 March 1993, no. 132-Rules for the Examination of the Applications for Registration of the By-Laws of Public Associations Active on the Territory of the Republic of Uzbekistan]

Zakon Respubliki Uzbekistan o mestnykh nalogakh i sborakh [Law of the Republic of Uzbekistan on Local Taxes and Payments], 7 May 1993, as amended 23 September 1994